THE MAD SCIENTIST'S

GUIDE

TO COMPOSITION

THE

MAD

SCIENTIST"S

GUIDE
TO COMPOSITION*

(A Somewhat Cheeky but Exceedingly Useful
Introduction to Academic Writing)

*now with 100% more monsters!

JEFFREY ANDREW WEINSTOCK

broadview press

BROADVIEW PRESS – www.broadviewpress.com
Peterborough, Ontario, Canada

Founded in 1985, Broadview Press remains a wholly independent publishing house. Broadview's focus is on academic publishing; our titles are accessible to university and college students as well as scholars and general readers. With over 600 titles in print, Broadview has become a leading international publisher in the humanities, with world-wide distribution. Broadview is committed to environmentally responsible publishing and fair business practices.

Library and Archives Canada Cataloguing in Publication

Title: The mad scientist's guide to composition* : a somewhat cheeky but exceedingly useful
    introduction to academic writing : *now with 100% more monsters! / Jeffrey Andrew
    Weinstock.
Names: Weinstock, Jeffrey Andrew, author.
Description: "Not as seen on TV." | Includes bibliographical references and index.
Identifiers: Canadiana (print) 20190170026 | Canadiana (ebook) 20190170034 | ISBN
    9781554814459 (softcover) | ISBN 9781770487239 (PDF) | ISBN 9781460406793
    (HTML)
Subjects: LCSH: Academic writing—Handbooks, manuals, etc. | LCSH: Report writing—
    Handbooks, manuals, etc. | LCSH: English language—Rhetoric—Handbooks,
    manuals, etc. | LCGFT: Handbooks and manuals.
Classification: LCC LB2369 .W45 2019 | DDC 808.02—dc23

Broadview Press handles its own distribution in North America:
PO Box 1243, Peterborough, Ontario K9J 7H5, Canada
555 Riverwalk Parkway, Tonawanda, NY 14150, USA
Tel: (705) 743-8990; Fax: (705) 743-8353
email: customerservice@broadviewpress.com

Distribution is handled by Eurospan Group in the UK, Europe, Central Asia,
Middle East, Africa, India, Southeast Asia, Central America, South America, and the
Caribbean. Distribution is handled by Footprint Books in Australia and New Zealand.

Canada

Broadview Press acknowledges the financial support of the
Government of Canada for our publishing activities.

Edited by Tania Therien
Book design by Michel Vrana

PRINTED IN CANADA

CONTENTS

MONSTERS ARE SCARY BUT WRITING DOESN'T HAVE TO BE!

I KNOW WHY YOU'RE HERE.

YOU ARE HERE BECAUSE THERE IS *NOTHING* YOU'D RATHER do than polish your writing skills, am I right?

Good, we're on the same page. (Both literally and figuratively.)

And I know that your being here has absolutely nothing to do with the course being a requirement.

Nope, certainly not.

You are *obviously* here because you *love writing* and would have taken this course under any circumstances. In fact, like most students, I have no doubt you were chomping at the bit to take freshman English (or the equivalent—your situation may vary).

Also, because you are obviously highly intelligent (as well as good looking), I can tell that you are the sort of person who appreciates that knowing the difference between

"Let's eat, Grandma!"

and

"Let's eat Grandma!"

can save lives—and I know you don't want Grandma's death on your hands (if only because you need to save that card to play when you forget about your Chemistry midterm. But I didn't say that).

We get each other. It's refreshing to meet a kindred soul.

But here's the weird thing. And I know you are going to find this hard to believe, but there are actually some people who aren't crazy about writing. Weird, huh?

Why is that? Well, yes, we do have to acknowledge that writing takes effort. As with acquiring any other skill, writing takes practice and patience. No one starts off knowing how to do a triple axel or to play guitar like Hendrix. Some people have more natural aptitude for skating or guitar (or both, I suppose—although not many people play guitar while skating; however, I can think of one memorable instance of a guy strapped to the front of a truck playing a fire-shooting guitar), but both are talents honed over time through paying attention to how others do it, practicing, getting feedback, and making adjustments—and one involves falling on your butt repeatedly until you get it right, while the other initially results in blistered fingers.

Writing is like that too, except you are, in most cases, less likely to literally fall on your butt or bleed from your fingers. In most cases.

But the fear and dread many people experience when it comes to writing often goes much deeper than laziness—because, after all, you are more than willing to put time and effort into things you find fun, rewarding, or valuable.

So why don't people find writing fun, rewarding, or valuable?

If you'll pardon my getting all academic for a minute, a researcher named Deborah Brandt did a study where she found that people generally had positive associations with reading. Some had favorite books growing up or remembered being read to by parents or teachers.

But writing was a different story. The people Brandt surveyed associated writing with "loneliness, secrecy, and resistance" (461). Many recalled writing as a chore, and some even remembered getting in trouble for it (writing on something they shouldn't have, such as walls or books, writing profanity or graffiti, etc.—nothing you've ever done, I'm sure). In few cases did Brandt's survey participants remember writing as something done together with others, emphasized by families, or something for which they were praised.[1]

---

1   If this interests you, you can check out the complete article: Deborah Brandt, "Remembering Writing, Remembering Reading," (continued)

A lot of the dread people feel about writing though is connected with how writing is introduced and taught to kids—and this is why, as you've no doubt anticipated, I'm now going to ask you to write a 15,000-word essay on the history of the tax code operating in your state or region. It will be worth 200 per cent of your semester grade, and you will lose 5000 points for each misplaced comma. Also, it was due yesterday. Also, it can only have three paragraphs. Ready?

I'm kidding, of course (or am I? If you think I'm kidding, turn to page 82. If you think I'm serious, please direct a check in the amount of $2000 to the author, care of the English department at Central Michigan University). But this is what I mean about the educational system being implicated in fostering a negative attitude toward writing. Students are often directed to compose essays around topics distant, shall we say, from their interests, the stakes are high, expectations are rigid, and the feedback mostly negative. The result? Anxiety and dread, of course.

College Composition and Communication, vol. 45, no. 4, 1994, pp. 459–79.

YOUR TURN

So have I nailed it or am I full of it? Write me a letter in which you describe your associations with writing and where they came from. If you have anxieties about writing, why? And what in your opinion would help you work through them? (And remember: if you tell me I'm totally full of it, then this assignment is worth fifty billion points. Just kidding ... maybe. [If you think I'm kidding, turn to page 82.])

IN THE WORDS OF EVERY INFOMERCIAL EVER: *THERE HAS TO BE A BETTER WAY!* AND, EUREKA! THERE IS! (OK, SORT OF.)

Yes, writing takes effort, but any task is made easier when you like what you're doing, get praised for it, and feel that you are improving. (And if you honestly recognize that you are honing a skill that can enrich your life and prevent grandma cannibalism, so much the better!)

AND THIS IS WHY IT IS NOW MY GREAT PRIVILEGE TO WELCOME YOU INTO THE FOLD OF THE INTERNATIONAL ORDER OF MAD SCIENTISTS!

Well done to you! Remember when Dr. Seuss told you Oh! The Places You'll Go? Well, you might not have foreseen ending up in a dusty laboratory (that's pronounced Lah-BORE-a-TOR-ee. You have to get it right now that you are a mad scientist) surrounded by beakers, potions, and brains in vats, but life takes strange paths, doesn't it?

SO NOW WE ARE GOING TO DO WHAT MAD SCIENTISTS DO: CONDUCT FORBIDDEN EXPERIMENTS!

READY TO START DIGGING?

It occurs to me that some of your classmates may now be thinking, "Umm ... huh?"

For their benefit (not yours—smart and good looking as you are, you've already figured this out), let me explain.

At this point in your academic career, the response is likely deeply conditioned—your instructor tells you to "compose an essay on ..." or "write a term paper," and what happens? Instant dread, anxiety, panic, fatigue, sometimes screaming, and possibly drooling.

The author, pictured here, demonstrates typical response to term paper assignment.

Experiments

Experiments on the other hand (especially forbidden ones): well, those are a different kettle of brains.

With an experiment, you *try things out and see what happens*. And as every mad scientist worth their salt knows, no matter how diligently one prepares, sometimes the monster lives, sometimes not so much. One hopes the lab doesn't blow up, but there is no expectation of success the first time around. The usual process is try, fail, tweak, try again. Repeat as needed.

So, fellow mad scientists, we are going to engage in monster building and conduct some "writing experiments." These will be experiments designed to introduce you to different types of academic writing of course (you are a scientist after all), and help you polish composition skills you'll need in other contexts (both academic and non-), but the idea is to think of them as experiments—that is, as opportunities to try out different styles of writing with no expectation of mastery the first or fifth or tenth time around.

There is another goal here however—one connected to mad scientists and monsters—and this is to try to have a bit of fun with writing. Let us combat the dread of writing by writing about dreadful things! Because if we can't have fun when writing about mad scientists, monsters, and the living dead, then all is lost. (However, since it might just be possible that this isn't everyone's kettle of body parts, there will be other options presented for the squeamish as well.)

A User's Guide to *The Mad Scientist's Guide*

Before we really get going, let me just say a little bit about how this book is set up because, believe it or not, there is a method to my madness here. This book consists of seven chapters that are sequenced in terms of the writing process: getting ready to write, organizing one's thoughts and planning, doing experiments, and then going back to the drawing board to tweak the experiment and try again. Chapter Six provides details about the most common systems of citation, and then I supply a few annotated examples of different types of student writing.

That said, the first thing you learn in mad scientists' school is that mad scientists seldom follow the rules—that's one thing that differentiates mad scientists from the more pedestrian sane ones. What that means is that *there is no need to work with this book in the order in which things are presented.*

While your instructor has the final say on things like this (remember this!), starting with Chapter One on mechanics—the subject most inclined to inspire nightmares—may not always be the best strategy. Mad scientists often operate on the "when all else fails, consult the instructions" premise.

It is also worth mentioning that this guide is filled with pop culture references and my tone is occasionally (OK, mostly) sarcastic. These things don't always translate well (which is one reason we now have emojis), so I'll do my best to clarify as we go along. If you think I'm being humorous though, you're probably right.

So the question then arises: How best to read and work with this guide?

1. Let your instructor guide you; they are the boss. That's why they get paid the big bucks.
2. Try to have fun with it! That's the point here. If you are writing and enjoying it, then we've won.
3. Remember that experiments sometimes crash and burn. That's the nature of experiments. Aim for success, but be ready to try again.

4. Think about what questions you have. Ask those questions. Don't say something or someone is unclear if you haven't asked for a clarification.

5. Write in this book. (Although if this is an ebook, then maybe don't write on your reader or computer. Especially if it isn't yours.) Write all over this book. Add moustaches to pictures as needed. Trust me—you aren't going to get much for selling this book back, so make it yours.

6. Use this book for other purposes such as killing flies and as a coaster. Get your money's worth out of it. But keep it handy. Refer to it.

7. Bear in mind that most of the essay examples included in this guide have been composed by undergraduates for particular courses. They shouldn't be presumed to be perfect. Users of this guide are encouraged to discuss their strengths and weaknesses.

8. And feel free to send me feedback (instructors too). If you ended up with a very successful assignment, found a mistake, have a suggestion for a revision or an additional assignment, you can direct them to **madscientistsguide@gmail.com**. Who knows? Maybe your essay on Slender Man or serial killers will end up in a future edition.

So, what do you think—are we good here?
If so, let's go!

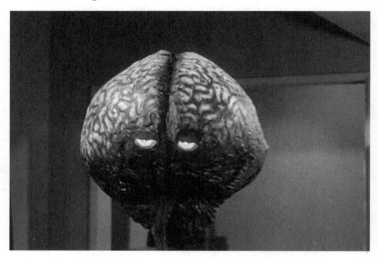

The author, figured here, excited to begin.

CHAPTER 1

NUTS AND BOLTS

(Mechanics)

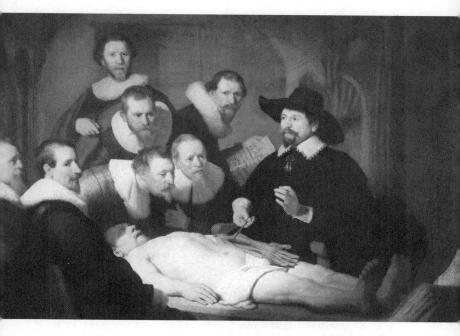

IT IS A FACT UNIVERSALLY ACKNOWLEDGED THAT YOU can't build a monster out of parts of corpses if you don't know how the bits and pieces go together. (We've all been there, right?)

The same goes for experiments in writing: if you want to be able to shout "It's alive!" at the end with thunder and lightning crashing around you, and then unleash your creation upon an unsuspecting world while you sit back and laugh maniacally, you need to start by getting the basic building blocks right. Because if your monster's got a foot for a head and no lungs, it isn't going to get too far and the other monsters will make fun of it. And then you have a sad, sad monster.

That's what this chapter is for: to refresh you on the basics of English prose anatomy and demon summoning as we prepare for our forbidden experiments in monsterpaperology.

YOUR TURN: THE HORROR, THE HORROR!

This section of the *Guide* on the "nuts and bolts" addresses the part of writing that often terrifies people the most. So what can we do about that?

Compose an entry for a *Mad Scientist's Diary* that explains what scares you the most about writing. What anxieties do you have? How have your experiments gone awry in the past? And what do you think will be the best ways to move forward with your experiments?

Here are two important things to bear in mind as we move forward here:

1. There is a big difference between mistakes that impact *meaning* and those that tend instead to signal a lack of polish. Yes, we want polished prose that shows an awareness of context, audience, and the conventions that go along with both, but the real focus needs to be on *conveying ideas clearly.*
2. Learning to write well and clearly is an ongoing process, not something that one masters all at once. As I discuss in Chapter Five on peer reviewing, even professional authors have editors!

Let's also be clear about one other thing: although you no doubt are the sort of highly intelligent and good-looking person who appreciates brushing up on the nuts and bolts of English prose, some people find such discussions a bit dry. That's where the monsters come in. So, let's start with ...

I. Dismembered Parts of Speech

This chipper fellow above is a monster, and monster is an example of a **noun**. *Nouns are words that identify a person, place, or thing.*

In the sentence, "The monster ate my brother," *monster* and *brother* are nouns. (Another way to think of nouns is as the things that either do something in a sentence or have something done to them—who eats or gets eaten. See "Grandma" in the introduction.)

Now this handsome fellow is of course Godzilla. And what is he doing? Clearly, he is *smiling* (duh). Smiling is a **verb**—verbs are words that describe what a person or thing does, or what happens.

In the sentence, "The cannibal feasted on the still-beating heart of his enemy," *feasted* is the verb—it is what the cannibal (the subject of the sentence) did to his enemy.

Now, let us turn our attention to blasphemous, pusillanimous, cacophonous adjectives with some help from our old friend, the mummy.

Adjectives are words that describe a noun. In the sentence, "The mummy shambled forth in moldering bandages from his dank, putrid tomb," the words *moldering*, *dank*, and *putrid* are adjectives. "Moldering" (which means decaying) modifies or describes the bandages, while "dank" and "putrid" describe the tomb.

This then brings us to the enigmatic **adverb**. While adjectives give us more information about a noun, adverbs give us more information about a verb, adjective, or other adverb. Adverbs tell us how something was done, where or when an action occurred, or the extent to which something was done.

In the sentence, "The brightly sparkling vampire was quickly staked," *brightly* and *quickly* are adverbs. In each case, they are words that modify a verb: "brightly" tells us about the absurd sparkling, while "quickly" tells us about the blessed staking (and both "absurd" and "blessed" are also adverbs here).

One other part of speech we need to address here, because they will become important later, are what are called **coordinating conjunctions**. These are words that can be used to connect independent clauses. The seven main ones in English are *for, and, nor, but, or, yet,* and *so.*

You can remember these with the acronym **FANBOYS**.

YOUR TURN:
MAD-LIBBING MONSTER STYLE

Supply the required part of speech to complete the phrase.
(And remember, kids: Victor says "keep it clean!")

All _____ and no _____ makes Jack a _____ _____.
   noun   *noun*   *adjective* *noun*

I _____ _____ people.
 verb   *adj*

This is no _____! This _____ is happening!
       noun   *adverb*

We all _____ a _____ crazy _____
      verb   *adverb*   *adverb*

I _____ his _____ with some _____ a nice _____.
 verb   *noun*   *noun*   *noun*

I have come here to _____ _____ and _____ _____ ...
             verb *noun*   *verb* *noun*

and I'm all out of _____.
           noun

_____ _____ is better.
adverb   *adjective*

The _____ of _____ compels you.
   noun   *noun*

Do you have _____ _____ to find _____...
       verb (infin.) *noun*   *noun*

to fall in love with?

You're going to _____ a bigger _____.
       verb   *noun*

II. I Am Legion: The Singular They

Grammatical rules of the past used to specify that generic or indeterminate nouns be referred to as "he"—using the singular masculine pronoun—as well as by the possessive "his."

For example:

- The *author* sold *his* soul to the devil. *He* achieved great fame, but at what cost?
- *Somebody* forgot *his* table manners!

The thinking on this matter, however, has shifted in the twenty-first century. While the use of "he" is still sometimes used to refer to a generic or indeterminate antecedent (a word replaced by a pronoun such as he), it has become much more common—and acceptable—to use "they" and "their" in such situations to be gender neutral.

Whereas it used to be considered proper grammar to write, "The alchemist mixed *his* chemicals," it is now acceptable to write, "Any alchemist should be careful when mixing their chemicals."

III. The Curious Case of the Incomplete Clause

Step one in creating a monster is to gather the materials you need: a genius's brain, an athlete's body, the face of an angel. Step two is to put the pieces together.

The same goes for creating a sentence. Step one: get some words (hopefully good ones). Step two: put them together.

What happens when you put words together into meaningful expressions is that you get **claws** (sometimes also spelled by the less imaginative as *clauses*). This can get complicated very quickly, but we are going to keep it simple here by focusing on two types of clauses: *independent clauses* and *dependent clauses*.

The werewolf howled at the moon.

"The werewolf howled at the moon" is an example of an *independent clause* (with claws!). An independent clause has a subject (a person, place, thing, or idea that is doing or being something) and a verb, and expresses a complete thought. In our example above, the werewolf is the subject of the sentence. "Howled" is the verb.

What's important for our purposes is that an independent clause is a *sentence*—a set of words complete in itself. If you've got **independent claws**, you are ready to slash and burn and take on the world!

When the moon emerged from behind the clouds ...

The poor *dependent clause*, however, isn't ready to slice and dice on its own because it doesn't express a complete thought. Consider the phrase, "When the moon emerged from behind the clouds." Well, what? What happened? Did some dude transform into a werewolf? Did a bat fly across the sky? Did an alien ship appear? We don't know because the thought is unfinished.

Dependent clauses are often signaled by what we pleasantly can refer to as:

DANGER WORDS

Danger words set up the first part of a two-part expression, and include:

after	since
although	though
as	unless
as if	until
because	whatever
before	when
even if	whenever
even though	whether
if	while
in order	

Here are a few examples of the immense peril created by danger words:

When the banshee wailed ... *(OK ... What happened?)*

Since the amulet is cursed ... *(don't wear it to dinner parties? It causes hives? It makes you ultra-sexy? What?!!!)*

Before summoning demons ... *(tidy up? Walk the dog? Reconsider?)*

The point here is that, in each case, these thoughts are incomplete. The danger words set up the first part of a two-part thought. By themselves, they aren't complete sentences. Instead, they are *sentence fragments*—sharp stabby shards of sentences that foil writing experiments.

YOUR MISSION (WHICH I WOULD ADVISE YOU TO ACCEPT) IS TO AVOID INCOMPLETE THOUGHTS (AKA SENTENCE FRAGMENTS, AKA DEPENDENT CLAUSES) IN YOUR WRITING BECAUSE ...

You can usually fix sentence fragments by either *combining* the dependent clause with another clause to make a complete sentence OR by removing the danger word:

When the banshee wailed, <u>we shuddered in fright</u>.

The amulet is cursed. *(We deleted the "since" here at the start.)*

Before summoning demons, <u>silence your cell phone</u>.

Before we leave the subject of *sentence formation errors of the damned*, let's talk about one other issue that has foiled many a mad scientist—and that is knowing when to stop.

If a sentence fragment is a short stabby section of a sentence that stabs meaning in the heart, its opposite is that monstrous abomination and thwarter of logic: the *fused sentence*. These are sometimes also called "run-on" sentences, but a better expression might be "run-away sentences"—as in run-away trains of words that leave your meaning flattened into mush.

Consider the following, which refers to the film *Halloween*:

Some said Jason only needed a hug, but they were wrong he was evil to his core.

What's happened here is that some truly insane mad scientist has created an unholy union of two independent clauses—two complete thoughts, each of which can stand on its own. "Some said Jason only needed a hug, but they were wrong" is an independent clause. It can stand alone. But so is "He was evil to his core." When you run them together as above, you create a fused sentence, and then Jason gets very, very angry.

In this case, there are three ways to fix this: with a period, semicolon, or a conjunction.

- Some said Jason only needed a hug, but they were wrong. He was evil to his core.
- Some said Jason only needed a hug, but they were wrong; he was evil to his core.
- Some said Jason only needed a hug, but they were wrong because he was evil to his core.

We'll talk about this in the next section. What's important here is that a *fused sentence* or *run-on sentence* is a mechanical error created when two independent clauses are combined. When you do this, Jason gets angry.

IV. Punctuation of Doooommmmmm

If you are going to build a monster out of words, punctuation will serve as the connective tissue. Little marks like periods, commas, and the poor, neglected apostrophe work to clarify meaning, as well as the relationships between words and sentences.

> She had broken Victor's heart so he stole a replacement and got back to business.

It is true that sometimes punctuation errors aren't a big deal. The sentence, "She had broken Victor's heart so he stole a replacement and got back to business" still makes sense without the comma that should technically precede the coordinating conjunction "so."

In other situations, though, using punctuation correctly is crucial to conveying your intended meaning. There is in fact a big difference between these two sentences (a variant on the "let's eat grandma!" scenario delightfully referenced in the introduction):

- Victor's passions include cooking his family and his dog.
- Victor's passions include cooking, his family, and his dog.

So in order to protect grandmas, families, and dogs everywhere, we'll run through the basics.

A. This Is the End

There are three ways to signal that the end has come—at least the end of a sentence: a **period**, an **exclamation mark**, and a **question mark**. Zombies aren't usually much help with anything, but they can help us with this.

A period marks the end of a statement: *The zombie ate Thurston.* The period tells us that the thought is complete.

However, let's say we actually care about Thurston, who was always a pretty decent guy, if a bit dim-witted. Then we might wish to show stronger emotion. For that, we use an exclamation mark: *Oh no! The zombie ate Thurston!* We might also use an exclamation mark to signal a sharp command: "Run!" (Alternatively, we might also use lots of exclamation points to complain about the picture of the zombies above.)

If, however, we are in shock and disbelief, and can't quite process that Thurston is gone, we would use a question mark to show uncertainty and to ask for more information: *What? Did a zombie really eat Thurston? Are you joking? Why would you joke about something like this? What is your problem? You are a sick, sick person!*

B. The Comma: Look upon Me and Despair

Of all the monsters included in this guide, few inspire such fear as the comma. Tiny splinters inserted into the hearts of sentences, but where? When? Oh, the horror, the horror! Part of the problem with commas is that they get used in a lot of different situations. Some of these are relatively straightforward (like in numbers and dates), some less so. We'll start with the tough ones.

1. Use commas to separate independent clauses joined by a coordinating conjunctions: *and, but, for, or, nor, so, yet.*

   The Kraken emerged from the briny depths, and not a man was spared to tell the horrid tale.

The sentence, "The Kraken emerged from the briny depths, and not a man was spared to tell the horrid tale," consists of two independent clauses, each of which could stand alone: "The Kraken emerged from the briny depths" and "Not a man was spared to tell the horrid tale." Were they run together without a comma or coordinating conjunction, the result would be a fused sentence: "The Kraken emerged from the briny depths not a man was spared." One way to avoid this is to insert a comma after the first independent clause, followed by a coordinating conjunction.

2. Use commas in the middle of a sentence to set off clauses, phrases, and words that are not essential to the meaning of the sentence.

The ghoul, whose name was Carl, could never figure out how to work the copy machine.

In the sentence above, "whose name was Carl" serves as a sort of aside—an extra bit of information that isn't necessary for the sentence to make sense. As a consequence, it is set off with commas.

THAT VS. WITCH (OR RATHER WHICH)

Without getting too technical here, don't put a comma before *that*. (Clauses with "that" are always considered essential.)

- The minotaur is a beast with a bull's head and a man's body that lives in a labyrinth.

Do put a comma before *which*

- The minotaur, which lives in a labyrinth, is a beast that has a bull's head and a man's body.

COMMAS AROUND TITLES?

When should you set off the title of a book, film, story, and so on with commas? Here's a rule of thumb that can work in most cases: **NO SENSE = NO COMMAS**

If you can delete the name of the work and the sentence still makes sense, set it off with commas. If you delete the name of the work and the sentence no longer makes sense, then no commas are needed:

- In Mary Shelley's novel, *Frankenstein*, the mad scientist's name is Victor.

In this case, you could delete *Frankenstein* and the sentence still makes sense: *In Mary Shelley's novel, the mad scientist's name is Victor*. Hence, set off the title with commas.

- Victor is the mad scientist in *Frankenstein* by Mary Shelley.

Here, if you deleted *Frankenstein*, you'd end up with *Victor is the mad scientist in by Mary Shelley*. Since that makes no sense, no commas are needed.

NO SENSE = NO COMMAS

3. Use commas after an introductory word or phrase at the beginning of a sentence.

Because her appearance turned people to stone, Medusa was unpopular at parties.

In this case, the comma separates the dependent clause, "Because her appearance turned people to stone," from the independent clause that follows.

The situation is the same with any kind of introductory phrase such as *Yes, mermaids love clam dip* and *Beware, the sun is rising!* In these examples, "Yes" and "Beware" are the introductory words.

4. Use commas near the end of a sentence for "afterthoughts"—words or phrases that follow the main clause.

You'll stay for dinner, won't you?

The "won't you?" above is set off from the main clause and follows a pause, so a comma precedes it.

5. Use a comma to shift between your language and a quotation.

A famous line from the film version of *Dracula* that isn't present in the novel is, "I never drink ... wine."

This one is a little tricky. In general, use a comma to introduce quoted material or dialogue. In the example here from *Dracula*, the comma preceding the quotation signals a shift in voice. It is no longer the author speaking, but a quotation from film.

However, skip using the comma if the quotation is introduced by a **conjunction** such as "that," "whether," or "if." In the sentence, *Dracula in the film quips that "I never drink wine,"* no comma is needed.

6. Use commas to separate three or more items in a list.

In preparing to do battle with the vampire, our heroes equipped themselves with holy water, wooden stakes, the communion wafer, and the Holy Hand Grenade of Antioch.

7. Use commas to separate two or more adjectives that describe the same noun.

As the coffin opened, the foul, fetid, acrid stench made their noses burn and their eyes water.

Here, foul, fetid, and acrid all describe the stench.

8. Use commas to set off all geographical names, items in dates (except the month and day), addresses (except the street number and name), and titles in names.

- Robert Louis Stevenson, the author of *The Strange Case of Dr. Jekyll and Mr. Hyde*, was born in Edinburgh, Scotland, on November 13, 1850.
- Within the novel, Henry Jekyll, MD, experiments on himself, which is seldom a good idea.

THE DREADED COMMA SPLICE

The bane of English instructors everywhere, the dreaded comma splice is a mechanical error created by using a comma inappropriately to yoke together two independent clauses—two complete thoughts each of which can stand alone. Here's an example:

> The phantom suddenly appeared before us, then she glided down the stairs and through the door.

"The phantom suddenly appeared before us" is a complete sentence. So is "Then she glided down the stairs and through the door." Because each of these is an independent clause, they can't be joined with just a comma.

There are three ways to fix this:

1. Use a period. The phantom suddenly appeared before us. **Then** she glided down the stairs and through the door.
2. Use a coordinating conjunction and a comma. The phantom suddenly appeared before us, **and** then she glided down the stairs and through the door.
3. Use a semicolon. The phantom suddenly appeared before us; then she glided down the stairs and through the door.

Speaking of semicolons ...

C. The Mysterious Semicolon

Semicolons are mysteries.

Legend has it, they arrived together with the aliens who built the pyramids. Cats are said to be fond of them, and it is whispered that Ponce de León, the Spanish conquistador who sought the Fountain of Youth in the fifteenth century, had one tattooed behind his ear. (All of this is true—just ask the Internet, where nothing untrue is permitted.) Can the semicolon bestow longevity upon you? Who knows! But definitely not if you use it incorrectly. Here is how to do it right.

A semicolon can be used to join two independent clauses (two sentences) when a coordinating conjunction is omitted or when they are linked by a transitional expression. As the "remember this rule" box below makes clear, the key part here is *independent clause*. What appears on each side of the semicolon needs to be a complete thought that can stand alone.

> **REMEMBER THIS RULE**: except when separating elements in a list, *don't use a semicolon where you couldn't substitute a period.*

1. The semicolon with two independent clauses, but without a coordinating conjunction

Many wonder if there is intelligent life on other planets; I often wonder if there is intelligent life on this one.

Here we have an example of the semicolon used to link two independent clauses (and, of course, in no way representative of the true feelings of the author). The semicolon separates sentences that have a close connection, but each of which can stand alone.

2. The semicolon with a transitional expression

The alien said he had come in peace; **however**, the ominous probe in his hand suggested less benign intentions.

Let's talk transitional expressions. Earlier, we went over *coordinating conjunctions*. There are seven of them—for, and, nor, but, or, yet, and so. You can use these together with a comma to link two independent clauses.

But if you aren't using one of these, then using a comma will create a comma splice. A semicolon together with a transitional expression is one way to avoid this messy fate.

Here are some common transitional phrases:

accordingly	moreover
consequently	nevertheless
for example	nonetheless
furthermore	on the other hand
however	otherwise
in addition	so
in fact	therefore
meanwhile	thus

D. The Revenge of the Apostrophe

Pity the poor apostrophe, a casualty of the age of text messaging. All it ever really wanted to do was help us to know when something was possessed ... by something else. But it has become hardened by neglect, angry, and vengeful. The only way to prevent its wrath from being unleashed upon an unsuspecting world is to use it properly. I know this is a weighty burden, but can we count on you to save us all?

The mummy's manicure was the envy of her friends.

The apostrophe s ('s) indicates that we are talking about something the mummy owns or possesses: in this case, her lovely nails.

The aliens' ship left as suddenly as it arrived, taking their delightful salsa recipe with them.

If the subject is plural and ends with s, add an apostrophe only. *Aliens'* with the apostrophe following the noun signals more than one alien. If you write *The Alien's ship* with an apostrophe before the s, this indicates only one alien. Placement here makes an important difference!

Anubis's head is that of a dog or jackal.

Treat words that end in s the same as you would any other ending.

E. Colon-oscopy

If you are building a monster out of body parts, it will need to have a colon. If you are building a monster out of words, it might also have a colon. These colons are not the same—do not mistake them.

The colon as punctuation mark has three main uses:

1. Use a colon to introduce a list of items following an independent clause.

The creature from the black lagoon has some unusual features: gills, flippers, claws, and fins.

In this example, *The creature from the black lagoon has some unusual features* is an independent clause. It is complete by itself. A colon can then be used at the end to introduce a list of those features.

The creature from the black lagoon has: gills, flippers, claws, and fins is a common, but incorrect, use of the colon since *The creature from the black lagoon has* is not by itself a complete thought. To correct his, you would simply delete the colon: *The creature from the black lagoon has gills, flippers, claws, and fins.*

2. Use a colon between independent clauses when the second explains or illustrates the first.

Monsters can be found all around the world: the bunyip, for example, comes from Australia.

3. Use a colon to emphasize a single word or phrase at the end of a sentence. Here again, the colon must follow an independent clause.

As is well known, Martians want only one thing: salt water taffy.

F. Quotation Marks: The Summoning

Quotation marks signal an act of summoning—that is, they *mark* the fact that you are *quoting* someone else (see how that works?).

In the North American system of punctuation, quotations are marked with double quotation marks:

In Charles Dickens's *A Christmas Carol*, the ghost of Jacob Marley tells Scrooge, "You will be haunted ... by Three Spirits."

Although this is often the source of some confusion, in the North American system, commas and periods go inside quotation marks, even if they aren't part of the original quotation:

In Mary Shelley's *Frankenstein*, the creature issues an ominous warning to Victor, telling him, "I will be with you on your wedding night."

Note how the period after "night" comes before the closing quotation mark, not after. Here's how you can remember this:

IF YOU ARE *IN* NORTH AMERICA, THEN PERIODS AND COMMAS GO *INSIDE* QUOTATION MARKS.

But what about other punctuation? If a quotation includes a question mark or exclamation mark, retain it inside the quotation marks. This becomes the "terminal" punctuation for the sentence.

- Bob then asked, "But what about me?"
- Sheila replied, "Not everything is about you, Bob!"

All other punctuation is placed outside of the quotation marks:

- Which film includes the famous line, "I see dead people"?

YOUR TURN:
SENTENCES GONE MAD!

Identify the sentence formation errors below and correct where needed.

1. Sirens draw their victims from passing ships. Either by causing sailors to jump overboard or wreck their ships on the rocks.
2. The tale of the zombie originated from West African folklore. Where they dwelled in the borderlands of the Vodou religion.
3. If you were to walk out outside and see a man crawling around on all fours you would wonder what was wrong with him. Especially when there was no understanding

the differences between a common sickness and the work of the devil.

4. The fear of clowns has been around for decades, most have seen recent videos, possibly real or fake, of clowns in the woods chasing people, sometimes, with a weapon.

5. While some believed that vampires originated from suicide.

6. The term "boogeyman" is commonly defined as an imaginary being who is used to scare children, it is unclear where exactly the boogeyman originated from, since the tale has been mostly passed down through generations verbally.

7. Zombies have been commonly portrayed in films as nothing more than brainless creatures that eat anything that moves.

8. Although there have been many sightings of Big Foot.

9. Slender Man is a modern creation he is the product of the digital age, produced by the manipulation of images.

10. Horror movies about monstrous children strike a nerve with parents. Who have anxieties about their lack of control over their children.

How well did you do? Check the answers on pages 36–38.

YOUR TURN:
THE PARAGRAPH FROM HELL

Igor tries hard. He really does. But his writing leaves a good bit to be desired. Help Igor whip his memoirs into shape by serving as his copy editor. How many errors can you find?

> ### *from "My Life," by Igor*
>
> Did I work hard for Dr. Frankenstein? Yes in the beginning. He took me in when no one else would. Although he needed help. Thats the real reason. He didn't care about my hump. Because he wanted a slave. He would tell me 'Igor do this' and 'Igor do that'. 'Yes Master' I always replied and I did try at the start.
>
> I will never forget the night the creature came to life though, it was the storm to end all storms. The doctor was very excited: 'get up on the roof', he told me. 'What?' I replied, 'are you crazy?' I will get struck by lightning'. 'Then I will find another assistant' he said that really hurt my feelings. So I did what he said even though I was terrified the whole time and that is when I resolved; to help the creature get lose.

V. Paranormal Paragraphs

As we build our creature, cells become tissue, and tissue becomes organs. And as we build our textual monster, words become sentences, and sentences become **paragraphs.** *A paragraph is a group of sentences all connected by one main idea.*

There is no set number of sentences in a paragraph. However, in general you should:

- Avoid paragraphs that are only one or two sentences long.
- Avoid stringing together multiple short paragraphs (which makes for "choppy" reading).

- Avoid paragraphs that go on for more than a full page of your text (if you have a paragraph that starts on page two and ends on page four, odds are good you've changed focus one or more times in the middle!).

THE KEY RULE OF THUMB HERE IS: NEW TOPIC = NEW PARAGRAPH

The main idea organizing a paragraph is expressed by a **topic sentence**. While topic sentences can appear anywhere in a paragraph, they usually appear near the beginning. The topic sentence tells the reader what the paragraph is about. All the other sentences in the paragraph should relate back to the topic sentence. In the paragraph below, the topic sentence is underlined:

<u>Part of what makes the Blob so fascinating, besides its amorphous appearance, is the lack of specific information about its origins and motivation.</u> The movie never explains where the creature came from or why it feeds on humans. The Blob has no personality—no human traits whatsoever;

"it is merely a mass of unexplained protoplasm driven
to ingest living creatures, and does so in a very simple
fashion: it merely absorbs them into its own body" (Warren
119). The creeping red menace has sometimes been inter-
preted as an allegory of communism (Murdico 29), but no
proof exists that the screenwriter or director intended such
a reading.[1]

As is often the case, the topic sentence here is the first sentence of the paragraph. It announces that this paragraph will be
about the role of ambiguity in *The Blob* and how that keeps us
questioning what it means. The rest of the sentences then develop
this idea.

HOW MANY PARAGRAPHS?

Students often are taught strict rules of writing, such as,
academic essays should only have three or five paragraphs. Poppycock! As mad scientists, we don't play
by the rules! While sometimes academic writing is con-
strained by length (this assignment must be thee pages or
900 words or something like that), in most cases essays
should have *as many paragraphs as they need*. The main
thing is that each paragraph is focused, and that later
paragraphs build on earlier ones toward your conclusion.

---

1   This passage comes from D. Felton, "The Blob," *The Ashgate
Companion to Monsters and the Monstrous*, edited by Jeffrey Andrew
Weinstock, Ashgate, 2014, p. 55. The parenthetical citations within the
passage are references made by Felton to other sources.

VI. Cross Over, Children: Transitions

If a paragraph is a focused block of text—a group of sentences all clustering around one main idea announced in a topic sentence, how does one cross over from one paragraph to the next? The answer is **transitions**. Transitional devices shift us gently from one paragraph to another by showing us a type of relationship. The following table gives some examples of different types of relationships and transitions. Many others exist:

Similarity	similarly, likewise, also, connected to this, in the same way
Contrast	however, on the other hand, in contrast, on the contrary, despite this, while
Order and Time	next, then, finally, meanwhile, after, subsequently
Cause and Effect	accordingly, as a result, consequently, hence, therefore
Additional Support	additionally, furthermore, as well, equally important, further, in addition
Conclusion	ultimately, in essence, in conclusion, finally, in sum

Note how the transitions function in these excerpted paragraphs below:

One of the first poltergeist cases to be more widely disseminated into literature and eventually cinema was the Tennessee Bell Witch disturbance of 1817–21. Another was an Australian case that occurred in the town of Guyra, New South Wales, in 1921....

More recently has been the case of the so-called Enfield poltergeist of London, England, an incident that lasted for several months during 1977–78. A mother and her four children (ages seven to thirteen) experienced mysterious scuffling sounds, beds shaking, furniture sliding across the floors, and books and toys being flung around the rooms. The disturbances became increasingly violent....

Where film is concerned, the best-known example to center on poltergeist activity is undoubtedly the aptly named *Poltergeist* (Tobe Hooper, 1982), in which a family moves into a home in a new development only to be terrified by inexplicable phenomena. The disturbances begin with chairs and other objects moving around. But soon youngest daughter Carol Anne (Heather O'Rourke), who had secretly been communicating with indistinct voices emanating from the television set, is sucked through an inter-dimensional portal in her bedroom closet....

Another film series to feature poltergeist activity, ultimately attributing it to a demonic spirit, is *Paranormal Activity* (Oren Peli, 2007) and its prequels, *Paranormal Activity 2* (Tod Williams, 2010) and *Paranormal Activity 3* (Henry Joost, 2011).[2]

---

2   The excerpt is from Debbie Felton, "Poltergeist," *The Ashgate Encyclopedia of Literary and Cinematic Monsters*, edited by Jeffrey Andrew Weinstock, Ashgate, 2014, pp. 475–78.

Isolation Is Destructive
Olivia van Buskirk

Frankenstein is very much a story about seclusion, intimacy and wanting to connect with someone, to feel part of something bigger than ourselves. Many of the main characters in *Frankenstein* feel detached from the world at some part of the story. This detachment leads to a series of deaths, despair and grief blanketing the characters and leaving them questioning the good in the world. Despite the fact that there is so much death and despair throughout the novel, isolation is the most destructive element of *Frankenstein*.

Captain Walton dislikes his lack of friends and feels too intelligent to fully connect with his shipmates. He writes to his sister "I desire the company of a man who could sympathize with me; whose eyes would reply to mine. You may deem me romantic, my dear sister, but I bitterly feel the want of a friend" (Shelley 19). Later, Walton's ship becomes trapped in ice, leaving him stranded in the northern seas, alone and away from his family. All Walton wants is someone who understands him and can see eye to eye with him, something he did not have growing up. As time continues, Walton eventually feels more and more alone. Meanwhile his sailors are on the brink of a mutiny, threatening to destroy the journey Walton had planned.

It is isolation and loneliness that allow Victor to create his monster in the first place. Once he sets his eyes on the final goal of bringing something to life, Victor locks himself away from his friends and family, working tirelessly to create his monster and bring something to life. While describing Victor when he is creating the monster, Shelley writes, "My cheek had grown pale with study, and my person had become emaciated with confinement" (55). Victor is obsessed with bringing his monster to life and he will do whatever it takes to succeed, even if that means spending countless days and nights in isolation.

While recounting his tale to Victor, the monster expresses his loneliness and desire to feel included in the world, something that will never be possible because of his physical appearance. His appearance alone ostracizes him from the world and no matter how hard he tries, no one will be friendly towards him. He tells Victor "Everywhere I see bliss from which I alone am irrevocably excluded" (Shelley 103). Additionally, the monster shares stories of his time watching the lives of Felix, Agatha and their father, wanting nothing more than to reveal himself to them and feel included. When he finally does, the monster is rejected and outcast, left to live a life of more loneliness. Being alone pushes the monster even further into his anger and causes him to continue inflicting destruction on the world, but specifically onto Victor.

The characters who suffer most in Shelley's *Frankenstein* are the ones who are alone. Although the times have changed, Shelley's story still reflects a common fear within modern society. Perhaps we could all take a lesson from Victor and learn to be more compassionate and welcoming instead of pushing people away simply because they are different. It is easy to isolate those that are different than us, but situations can change and we can quickly become the isolated. Now, more than ever, is a time to practice empathy and compassion so hopefully people will never have to feel as lonely as Victor and his creation.

Sentences Gone Mad Answer Key

1. Sirens draw their victims from passing ships. Either by causing sailors to jump overboard or wreck their ships on the rocks.

"Either by causing sailors to jump overboard or wreck their ships on the rocks" is an incomplete thought (a sentence fragment). The easiest fix is to exchange the period after "passing ships" for a comma: "Sirens draw their victims from passing ships, either by causing sailors to jump overboard or wreck their ships on the rocks."

2. The tale of the zombie originated from West African folklore. Where they dwelled in the borderlands of the Vodou religion.

"Where they dwelled in the borderlands of the Vodou religion" is an incomplete thought (a sentence fragment). The quickest fix is to exchange the period after "folklore" for a comma: "The tale of the zombie originated from West African folklore, where they dwelled in the borderlands of the Vodou religion."

3. If you were to walk out outside and see a man crawling around on all fours you would wonder what was wrong with him. Especially when there was no understanding the differences between a common sickness and the work of the devil.

Two issues with this sentence: first, a comma is needed after "all fours." Second, "Especially when there was no understanding the differences between a common sickness and the work of the devil" is an incomplete thought (fragment). Fix this, as in 1 and 2, by changing the period after "him" to a comma.

4. The fear of clowns has been around for decades, most have seen recent videos, possibly real or fake, of clowns in the woods chasing people, sometimes, with a weapon.

The problem here is not with sentence fragments, but rather with a "comma splice"—a type of run-on sentence in which a comma is used to yoke together two independent clauses—complete thoughts—each of which can stand alone. To fix it here, follow "for decades" with a period and then make "Most" the start of a new sentence. Alternatively, follow "for decades" with a semicolon and keep "most" lowercase.

5. While some believed that vampires originated from suicide.

This is an incomplete thought (fragment). Note the danger word, "while," at the beginning. A second part to the sentence is needed. For example, "While some believed vampires originated from suicide, others claimed they were created by excommunication."

6. The term "boogeyman" is commonly defined as an imaginary being who is used to scare children, it is unclear where exactly the boogeyman originated from, since the tale has been mostly passed down through generations verbally.

Here we have a comma splice as two independent clauses have been yoked together creating a run-on sentence. Fix this by changing the comma after "children" to a period and capitalizing

"It." Alternatively, swap the comma after "children" for a semicolon and then leave "it" lowercase.

7. Zombies have been commonly portrayed in films as nothing more than brainless creatures that eat anything that moves.

This sentence is mechanically correct.

8. Although there have been many sightings of Big Foot.

This is an incomplete thought (fragment). Note the danger word, "although," at the beginning. A second part to the sentence is needed. For example, "Although there have been many sightings of Big Foot, he has never accepted a party invitation."

9. Slender Man is a modern creation he is the product of the digital age, produced by the manipulation of images.

Here we have a "fused sentence"—two complete thoughts run together, creating a run-on. To fix this, add a period after "modern creation" and then capitalize "He." Alternatively, insert a semicolon after "modern creation" and leave "he" lowercase.

10. Horror movies about monstrous children strike a nerve with parents. Who have anxieties about their lack of control over their children.

"Who have anxieties about their lack of control over their children" is a fragment. It does not express a complete thought. The simplest fix here is just to delete the period after "parents" and create one sentence: "Horror movies about monstrous children strike a nerve with parents who have anxieties about their lack of control over their children."

CHAPTER 2

GRAVEROBBING

(Finding, Evaluating, and Incorporating Sources)

WELCOME BACK, MY INTELLIGENT AND GOOD-LOOKING FRIENDS!

This chapter is about summoning spirits and graverobbing—that is, calling upon the voices of others and using them as a means to develop your own ideas (also known as "doing research"). Here we will focus on the three steps of the research process: *finding sources, evaluating sources,* and *incorporating sources* into your writing.

To kick things off, let's begin with one of the more embarrassing episodes in the later life of Victor Frankenstein, mad scientist extraordinaire. (I hasten to add that the following account is totally true. No names have been changed to protect anyone. *Totally true.*)

Victor had been invited to present his research on the reanimation of dead flesh at the annual mad scientist's convention in Las Vegas. The talk went well. Victor's PowerPoint was well received and bored no one (because no one is ever bored by PowerPoint). Victor was feeling quite pleased with himself ... until a colleague pointed out that the process claimed by Victor as his big breakthrough was the same one described in an article in the *Mad Scientist's Annual* two years earlier by Herbert West. Other parts of Victor's talk were then discovered to have been taken from other sources! Branded a plagiarist, Victor then had his membership in the Mad Scientist's Association revoked and was barred from the buffet. Bad Victor.

This is what is known in "the business" as a "cautionary tale." We are exploiting Victor's shame as an illustration of the potential consequences of sloppy research and citation practices. Paying careful attention to this chapter can not only help your experiments go smoothly, but keep you from ending up looking like—and sorry to get technical for a moment—a nincompoop who gets barred from the buffet.

So, here's the question: what's the point of doing research at all? (That is, apart from being forced by ridiculously mean instructors who fail to take into consideration that you have a life and that this isn't the only course you are taking, you know.)

Here are four justifications:

1. To avoid duplicating the results of others
2. To use the insights of others to help focus and develop one's own ideas
3. To find evidence to bolster one's claims
4. To demonstrate a command of the field of inquiry

Thorough research thereby helps to make sure that your experiment is one worth undertaking in the first place, helps to make sure it is successful, and helps to convince others that you know what you are talking about (thus making your writing more persuasive by establishing *ethos*, which we'll talk about in Chapter Four).

Conjuring Spirits: Finding and Using Sources

I. Some Terminology

Step 1 in the research process is "conjuring" useful sources **from beyond the grave**. Before we get to that though, a quick refresher on some vocabulary may be helpful.

PRIMARY VS. SECONDARY SOURCES

You've been assigned to come up with ten secondary sources on your topic. What's a secondary source anyway? And secondary as opposed to what?!

Let's say you've decided to research the windigo, the mythical cannibal monster described in Algonquian folklore that allegedly roams the northern forests of the Atlantic coast and

Artist's rendering of actual photo of a windigo.

41

Great Lakes region of North America munching on any hapless souls who cross its path.

Primary sources would be stories about and accounts of the monster. These could include Native American folktales, interviews with tribal members about local legends, perhaps even updated narratives about the windigo, such as Stephen King's novel *Pet Sematary*.

Secondary sources then would be non-fiction articles, essays, book chapters, books, and so on that interpret the primary sources.

> A *primary source* is something not interpreted for you by someone else. These may be creative works, or texts created by witnesses to or participants in some event.
> *Secondary sources* are sources that interpret, describe, or draw conclusions based on other sources.

Another example: say you decide to research the roles monsters play in the Harry Potter books and films. The books by J.K.

Fluffy, the three-headed dog, from Harry Potter and the Sorcerer's Stone *is an adaptation of Cerberus, the three-headed dog who guards the entrance to the underworld in Greek myth.*

Rowling and their cinematic adaptations would be your *primary sources*. In this case, *Harry Potter and the Chamber of Secrets* (book, movie, or both) could serve as a *primary source*.

Non-fiction articles, essays, book chapters, and books about the Harry Potter universe and/or about the kinds of monsters present in the books and films would be secondary sources. Secondary sources could include Peter Costello's *The Magic Zoo: The Natural History of Fabulous Animals* (which explores the possible origins of mythical creatures such as the basilisk) and the edited collection of scholarly essays on the Potterverse called *Reading Harry Potter: Critical Essays*.

SCHOLARLY VS. NON-SCHOLARLY SOURCES

When doing research, your goal should be to find *the most reliable, authoritative, appropriate, and useful sources possible* for your project—and the most reliable and authoritative ones are most likely to be *scholarly sources*.

Scholarly sources are ones written by experts, typically for others with a background in the subject. While experts are not always right, they are more likely to be right than someone without a background in the subject. Put differently, someone who has spent years researching a particular subject is more likely to know what they are talking about than someone who hasn't.

And what you are most likely really looking for when doing research are **peer-reviewed** scholarly sources, which are the "gold standard" for academic research.

> If something has been peer-reviewed, it means that it has been evaluated by experts in the field and approved by those experts as meriting publication.

Here is how peer-reviewing works on the professional level: imagine that Dr. Jekyll wishes to publish his research into the moral nature of humanity in the totally not-made-up academic journal, *Journal of the Moral Nature of Humanity* (seems a good fit, doesn't it?). Since this totally not-made-up journal maintains very high standards, they receive Dr. Jekyll's submission and immediately send it out to two **field readers**—experts in the subject matter. These readers then offer their evaluation of Dr. Jekyll's submission (which hopefully has been rendered anonymous), and may recommend that it be published as is, that it be sent back to Dr. Jekyll for revisions, or be rejected altogether. This system of peer reviewing helps to make sure that scholarship published in the journal is original and convincing.

The best sources for any research project are therefore *peer-reviewed scholarly sources*, which, unsurprisingly, are generally found in scholarly journals and books published by academic publishers. (We'll talk in "evaluating sources" below about how to know if something has been peer reviewed or not.)

OK, so if those are scholarly sources, what then are non-scholarly sources?

Non-scholarly sources are often authored by writers who are not experts in the subject matter being discussed. They are also often written for the general public, rather than for other experts in the field, and often appear in what is called **the popular press**—newspapers, magazines, and websites for non-experts.

So, let's imagine this time that, rather than Dr. Jekyll publishing his research in a journal catering to other experts in the field, a journalist writes an article about Dr. Jekyll and publishes it in the local newspaper. This article may contain a lot of useful information, but it is not considered scholarly.

For more differences between scholarly and non-scholarly sources, see the discussion of this distinction in the "evaluating sources" section below.

PERIODICALS AND JOURNALS

A periodical is a newspaper or magazine that comes out (surprise!) periodically—that is, at regular intervals. This may be daily, weekly, monthly, quarterly, etc.

A journal is a specific type of periodical focused on a particular subject or professional activity. *The Journal for the Fantastic in the Arts*, for example, is a scholarly periodical published three times a year that focuses on speculative literature and media (fantasy, science fiction, horror, and so forth). *The American Journal of Psychology* is a long-running journal focused on psychology. There are many professional journals.

Journals contain *essays* or *articles*. (While essays typically argue a thesis and articles typically are meant to inform, these terms are often used interchangeably.) So, if you cite a source found in a journal, you refer to it as a *journal essay* or *journal article*.

THE JOURNAL IS THE MAGAZINE ITSELF.

JUST WHAT THE HECK IS A NOVEL?

I include this here because I've noticed increasing confusion about this term among students who, from time to time, come in thinking any book is a novel.

So let's be clear:

A NOVEL IS A BOOK-LENGTH WORK OF *FICTION.*

Harry Potter and the Chamber of Secrets is a novel. Mary Shelley's *Frankenstein* is a novel. Bram Stoker's *Dracula* is a novel. Stephen King's *The Shining* is a novel. *The Hunger Games*: novel.

In contrast, a biography of Winston Churchill is *not* a novel. Your math textbook is *not* a novel. Elizabeth Kolbert's *The Sixth Extinction: An Unnatural History*, a book that explores the dramatic impact of human activity on the natural environment, is *not* a novel. Edgar Allan Poe's short story, "The Tell-Tale Heart," is *not a novel* because it is not the length of a book, and neither is his poem "The Raven."

If it is not fiction, it is not considered a novel. If it is not a book-length work, it is not considered a novel.

EDITORS AND EDITED COLLECTIONS

In some cases when doing research, you may come across what are called *edited collections.* An edited volume or edited collection is a book that collects together chapters *written by different authors. The editor is the person who has assembled the volume*; this person did not write all the chapters included in the book. What is important here is that you acknowledge the person who wrote the essay or article you are using for your research, not the editor. This is called

citing your source. To cite a source is to give credit to the author whose ideas and/or words you are using.

For example, I am the editor of an edited collection of scholarly essays called *Critical Approaches to the Films of Tim Burton: Margins to Mainstream*. If in your research, however, you came across Aaron Taylor's essay in this collection, "How to See Things Differently: Tim Burton's Reimaginings," you would cite Taylor in your works cited, not me. (More about this in Chapter Six.)

II. Burial Sites: Finding Sources

It's time to get down to business now. You've got a general topic in mind and want to start gathering sources on it. How to proceed?

An analogy may be helpful here. Let's say you've got a fantastic salsa recipe (given to you by the aliens mentioned in Chapter One) and need to get ingredients to make it, including fresh tomatoes, onions, and hot peppers—although you are not sure exactly what kind of peppers will be best (the aliens weren't terribly clear on this matter).

The available destinations for your shopping trip include:

1. An auto parts store
2. The super colossal mega-department store
3. The farmer's market (which includes a lady who sells various kinds of hot peppers and who is super nice and really knowledgeable)

Which do you choose? (If you choose the auto parts store, turn to page 98.)

Now, extensive research allows us to conclude with a high degree of probability that fresh produce is seldom available at auto parts stores, so you can probably rule that out.

And you might find fresh produce at the super-colossal mega-department store, but you might not. And even if you do, you might not find the best vegetables for your salsa recipe or someone who can help you decide among peppers. So the best choice (surprise!) turns out to be the local farmer's market.

The situation when doing research is the same: *you are looking for the best sources to assist with your project*. In order to find those sources, you need to identify the most relevant *databases and catalogs* for what you are doing. There are in fact many different databases that specialize in particular areas (see below).

And now, a very important tip:

DO *NOT* START AND END WITH A GOOGLE SEARCH

Google is the online search equivalent of the super-colossal mega-department store. You'll get millions of results. Will they be the best ones for your project? Probably not. Will the results include some sketchy ones? Pretty likely.

Let's say you decide you are interested in researching zombies in popular culture. A Google search of "zombies popular culture" nets "about 5,170,000 results"! And the top hits, while useful, aren't scholarly sources.

Rolling Stone, *BBC.com*, *LiveScience.com*, *Huffington Post*, and *Digitalspy.com* are all examples of popular press sources. They may be useful to you, but they aren't scholarly sources.

I am also now going to caution you about using the search box that may appear on your library's homepage. Here is why: at

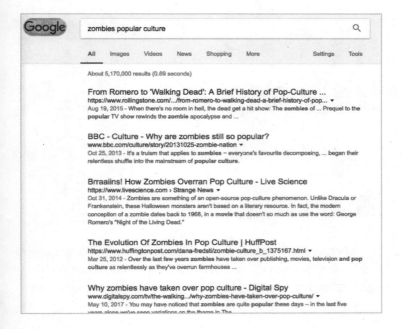

the university where I teach, the library website has a search box called "Smart Search."

If I enter "zombie" here, I get some results. A lot of results—64,417 results to be exact. And these results are of many different kinds: novels, articles, films, and so on. So this ends up being kind of like a Google search.

These results can be narrowed down in two ways. First, the results that come back after running the general search can be "tweaked." That is, the results can be sorted into different categories.

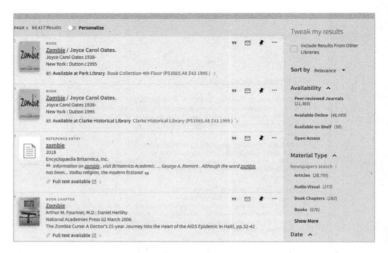

Another way to narrow down the results is by using a drop-down menu prior to the initial search. Rather than just running a generic search, another option is to look specifically for peer-reviewed articles.

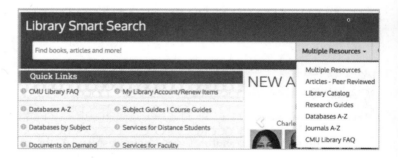

Running a search using "zombie" as a key word and selecting "articles – peer reviewed" narrows down the results ... somewhat. The result is now 10,056 results—and the results include many articles that, while interesting, are unlikely to be useful to you if you are writing about the living dead. So this ends up kind of being like a Google search.

So, what should you do? Go to the farmer's market to find fresh vegetables.

What I mean by this is that you'll have the best results by searching *database*s that are specific to the research you are doing.

Go back to the homepage for your library and look for a menu of databases. You might find something like this:

Showing 61 Subjects			
Anthropology	5	How To	30
Art	1	Interior Design	1
Arts & Humanities	18	Journalism	9
Biographies	1	Law	9
Biology	2	Legal Research	3
Broadcasting	7	MA in Ed Resources	15
Business (Companies)	3	Management	7

Selecting from the available options will help focus your searches.

But what if there are multiple options and you aren't sure which one to use?

Prepare yourself (are you ready?): what if I told you that there are people who are trained to assist you with this and are paid to do so?

BOOM! Did I just blow your mind?

Librarians in popular culture are typically represented as either incredibly sexy or monstrous, but, in reality, they mostly help people find the resources they need and only occasionally eat researchers.

A quick consultation with your friendly neighborhood librarian points you toward the MLA International Bibliography, a

database of scholarship on literature, film, and popular culture. A keyword search there using "zombies" yields 701 hits—a lot, but far less than five million or 10,000!

But here is where things get fun. If you look at the image above, you'll see that we can filter the results using "peer reviewed" as a criterion. When we do that, the total drops down to 207 results—still a lot, but getting closer to being manageable. And the bonus is that the results are now all peer-reviewed scholarly sources. Fun, right? I know!!!

STEP ONE:
CONSULT THE MOST APPROPRIATE
DATABASES FOR YOUR PROJECT.

STEP TWO:
FOLLOW ARIADNE'S THREAD.

In Greek mythology, the Minotaur was a fearsome creature with the head of a bull and the body of a man that lived at the center of a complex labyrinth. When the hero Theseus entered the labyrinth in pursuit of the monster, he unraveled a ball of thread given to him by the princess Ariadne as he went so that he could find his way out again.

Yes, yes, I hear you saying. What does this have to do with doing research?

Once you begin finding sources, there is a ball of thread you can follow to help you negotiate the labyrinth of research. *Scholarly sources always cite their sources* (this is one way you can distinguish scholarly sources from non-scholarly sources). So, if you find a scholarly source that works for your project, *look at its sources*. This can lead you to other relevant sources!

Let's go back to our MLA database search on zombies above. We ended up with 224 peer-reviewed results. Scrolling through the results, we hit on an essay called "Vampire Gentlemen and Zombie Beasts" by Angela Tenga and Elizabeth Zimmerman that was published in the scholarly journal *Gothic Studies* in 2013. This article ends up being very relevant to our project as it deals with *The Walking Dead*, *True Blood*, and *Twilight*. Looking at this essay's notes, what we discover are the sources consulted by Tenga and Zimmerman, many of which may also be relevant to our project:

Vampire Gentlemen and Zombie Beasts	85

2 Grossman, 'Zombies Are the New Vampires', para. 2 of 8.

3 Natalie Wilson, *Seduced by* Twilight (Jefferson, NC: McFarland, 2011), p. 16.

4 S. T. Joshi, *Ramsey Campbell and Modern Horror Fiction* (Liverpool: Liverpool University Press, 2001), p. 20.

5 Ken Gelder, 'Introduction', in *The Horror Reader* (London, Routledge, 2000), p. 4; James B. Twitchell, *Dreadful Pleasures: An Anatomy of Modern Horror* (Oxford: Oxford University Press, 1985), p. 92.

6 Nina Auerbach, *Our Vampires, Ourselves* (Chicago: University of Chicago Press, 1995), p. 3; Gregory Waller, *The Living and the Undead: Slaying Vampires, Exterminating Zombies* (Urbana: University of Illinois Press, 2010), p. 8.

7 Stephen D. Arata, '*Dracula* and the Anxiety of Reverse Colonisation', in Bram Stoker, *Dracula*, ed. Glennis Byron (Peterborough, ON: Broadview, 2000), pp. 119–44 at p. 125; Waller, *The Living and the Undead*, p. 40.

8 *Forever Knight*, created by James D. Parriott and Barney Cohen (Canada: CBS, 1989–1996).

9 *Dark Shadows*, created by Dan Curtis (USA: ABC, 1966–1971).

10 Craig Hamrick, *Barnabas and Company* (New York: iUniverse Publishing, 2003), p. 4.

11 Julia Kristeva, *The Powers of Horror: An Essay on Abjection*, trans. Leon S. Roudiez (New York: Columbia University Press, 1982), p. 4.

12 Kyle Bishop, *American Zombie Gothic: The Rise and Fall (and Rise) of the Walking Dead in Popular Culture* (Jefferson, NC: McFarland, 2010), p. 132.

13 See Glenn D. Walters, 'Understanding the Popular Appeal of Horror Cinema: An Integrated-Interactive Model', *Journal of Media Psychology*, 9:2 (2004), 1–35.

14 W. B. Seabrook, *The Magic Island* (New York: Literary Guild of America, 1929; repr. New York, Paragon, 1989), p. 97.

15 Kim Paffenroth, *Gospel of the Living Dead: George Romero's Visions of Hell on Earth* (Waco, TX: Baylor University Press, 2006), p. 1.

Looking at this essay's sources can lead us to other useful ones. In this way, we follow the thread from one source to the next.

There is an additional benefit of letting our sources direct us to other sources: *if the same source is cited repeatedly in several different places, this lets you know that it is an important source.*

A part of the research process is becoming conversant with the published scholarship in that area. This involves having a sense of the leading voices and central studies.

STEP THREE:
SUPPLEMENT YOUR SEARCHES OF RELEVANT SCHOLARLY DATABASES WITH SEARCHES OF GOOGLE OR OTHER GENERAL DATABASES AS DESIRED.

I'm not saying never make use of Google, just make sure that you utilize the most appropriate and useful resources first.

And a word to the wise: your instructor will look at your sources and with a quick glance will know whether you have skipped the scholarly database step and just gone with Google. It is really easy to see, because the sources you end up with are unlikely to be the best ones for any research project. *You've been warned! (Muhahahahahaha)*

Here Lies Truth: Evaluating Sources

We need to get serious for a moment.

A 2016 study conducted by researchers at Stanford University focused on the ability of students to evaluate the credibility of sources of information, and described the results as "'dismaying,' 'bleak' and '[a] threat to democracy.'" National Public Radio summarized the results:

> Middle school, high school and college students in 12 states were asked to evaluate the information presented in tweets, comments and articles. More than 7,800 student responses were collected. In exercise after exercise, the researchers were "shocked"—their word, not ours—by how many students failed to effectively evaluate the credibility of that information.[1]

In the era of social media echo chambers and fake news, critical thinking about the authoritativeness and reliability of sources is more imperative than ever and *it ultimately comes down to you to know who and what you are citing in your research.*

So how do you know if something is reliable or not? Here are some questions to ask:

1. Has it been peer reviewed?

As mentioned above, peer reviewing is the gold standard of scholarly publication. Many databases, like the MLA database, will allow you to refine searches to exclude anything that isn't peer reviewed. The homepages of many academic journals will make clear that peer reviewing is part of their publication process.

---

1   Camila Domonoske, "Students Have 'Dismaying' Inability to Tell Fake News from Real, Study Finds," *National Public Radio*, 23 November 2016, http://www.npr.org/sections/thetwo-way/2016/11/23/503129818/ study-finds-students-have-dismaying-inability-to-tell-fake-news-from-real.

Postmodern Culture

As the first electronic peer-reviewed journal in the humanities, *Postmodern Culture (PMC)* is a groundbreaking experiment in scholarly publishing. It has become a leading journal of interdisciplinary thought on contemporary cultures. *PMC* offers a forum for commentary, criticism, and theory on subjects ranging from identity politics to the economics of information. Subscriptions include access to all previous volumes of *PMC* in a comprehensive web-based interface with full-text searchability.

Editor

Eyal Amiran, University of California, Irvine

2. Who is the publisher?

University presses (like the University of Minnesota Press or Stanford University Press) and established commercial publishers of academic materials such as Palgrave, Routledge, and Bloomsbury can be relied upon to send manuscripts out for peer review. Again, looking at the homepage for a publisher can often help you evaluate the reliability and authoritativeness of the texts it publishes.

Non-scholarly popular press sources are more problematic because it is often unclear what kind of fact-checking or evaluation of materials has been performed. Major news sources such as *The New York Times* and *Washington Post* do their best to fact-check articles prior to publication, but other sources may be less scrupulous. And things like blogs and webpages may not be fact checked or have undergone any process of review at all.

The issue of publisher also dovetails with the vexed issue of **bias**.

> To *be biased* means to be prejudiced for or against something in a way that colors or undercuts objective evaluation of data. (*Bias* is a noun—it is something you have. If you have it, then you are *biased*.) Scholarly writing strives for objectivity—that is, it attempts to draw conclusions based on the data without allowing bias to influence the outcome.

The issue of bias in relation to media sources has received a good bit of attention in recent years. Several different charts have been developed to help media consumers assess the bias and reliability of different news content providers.

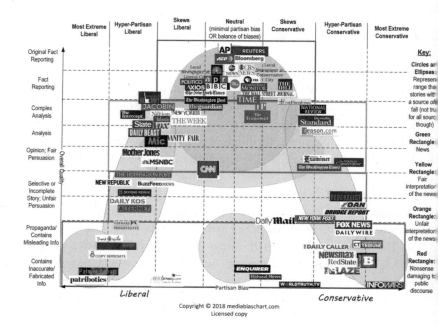

3. Who is the author?

Knowing who the author is of an article or essay can often help you evaluate how reliable the source is, because this can help establish the author's credentials for writing on the subject.

Many scholarly sources will include identifying information about the author. This information is often found on the backs of books, or in an "about the contributors" page in an edited collection or journal issue. Sometimes, journal essays include identifying information about the author at the beginning or end. For example, the "Vampire Gentlemen and Zombie Beasts" article mentioned above includes these capsule biographies at the end:

Knowing who an author is can also help you identify bias.

Notes on contributors

Angela Tenga gained her doctoral degree from Purdue University and currently teaches courses in literature, history, and popular culture at Florida Institute of Technology. Her research interests include early English literature and the literary monstrous, with emphasis on undead fiction, fictional serial killers, and representations of the medieval in modern popular culture. Her publications include 'Read Only as Directed: Psychology, Intertextuality, and Hyperreality in the *Twilight* Series' (2011) and 'Reformed Vampires from Forks to Florida' (2011).

Elizabeth Zimmerman is currently a doctoral student at Southern Illinois University, Carbondale. Her dissertation focuses on nineteenth-century American literature, with a

---

Vampire Gentlemen and Zombie Beasts   87

special interest in the American Gothic. She is a graduate of Bowling Green State University where she carried out postgraduate research on vampire literature, leading to an interest in this project. She has also attended several Popular Culture Association/American Culture Association conferences, presenting papers on immortality, evil, and vampire literature.

---

4. Does the source cite its sources clearly and completely?

A marker of authoritative scholarly writing is that it is scrupulous about citing its sources. It will clearly identify material taken from other sources in the body of the text, and then provide complete citations for sources in notes or a list of works cited or references at the end.

5. Is the source consistent with other sources?

If you have several sources that say one thing, and one source that says something different, approach the one that runs contrary to the consensus with care. Try to evaluate on what basis the author's claims are being made—and check to see what sources are cited by the author.

Sources of Despair

Approach these sources with care:

1. **Encyclopedia Articles**. Encyclopedia articles can be a good starting point for academic research, but avoid an overreliance on them. Encyclopedia articles are actually considered "tertiary sources." What they do is to offer a summary of primary and secondary sources on a topic. While generally considered scholarly, entries are in most cases reviewed by an editor or editorial board rather than being peer-reviewed.

   Allow encyclopedia articles to direct you to primary and secondary texts on your topic rather than to substitute for consulting primary and secondary sources. Relying primarily on encyclopedia articles rather than consulting more extensive and thorough sources is lazy researching!

2. **Book Reviews**. Like encyclopedia articles, book reviews can help you identify sources that will be useful to you. *If the book being reviewed seems helpful and relevant, get that book!* Don't quote someone quoting or describing the book. This also is lazy researching!

3. **Wikipedia.** You probably know this by now, but Wikipedia is not considered a scholarly or particularly reliable source because anyone can write and edit entries. As with encyclopedia articles in general, it can be very useful in supplying background and directing you to more authoritative and reliable sources.

4. **Academia.edu.** Academia.edu is the most prominent of several for-profit social networking websites that academics use for various reasons including to share research. Academics upload materials themselves

and can share whatever they like. This can range from published essays and book chapters to lecture materials to unpublished conference papers. *There is no guarantee anything you find here has been peer-reviewed or even published.* If you find something on academia.edu that seems useful, look to see if it has been published—and use the published version.

5. **Undergraduate and Graduate Theses and Dissertations.** In general, be wary of undergraduate Honors theses, graduate Masters theses, and Doctoral dissertations. These sources are written primarily for the faculty committee overseeing the project, are not peer-reviewed, and are not published in the conventional sense.

    If you find a PhD dissertation that seems useful, look to see if it has been published in part or in whole either as journal articles or a book. (It is often the case that a doctoral dissertation becomes a scholar's first book—usually after substantial revision.)

6. **Websites and Blogs.** These can be useful, but make sure you know who the author is as there is a big difference between citing a blog maintained by a published expert in a field and one created by a junior high school student for their history class.

One last point here: the burden falls on you to know who and what you are citing in your writing, and it is always unpleasant to have someone point out to you that a source you've used is suspect. Here, therefore, are some questions to ask about the sources you find, which we can group into four categories: *author, publication venue, currency,* and *reliability.*

QUESTIONS TO ASK

AUTHOR	Who is the author and what expertise do they hold? Is the author someone who has published widely on the subject? Is it a college student? Is it a journalist? Can you even determine who the author is? Is the author affiliated with an organization that might suggest bias?
	(Your Answer)
PUBLICATION VENUE	Where was the source published and who published it? Is it self-published? Is it a site to which anyone can contribute or upload? Is it a newspaper or news site? If so, does that site have an agenda or bias? Is the publisher an academic publisher? Does the publisher have a policy of peer review?
	(Your Answer)
CURRENCY	How recent is the source? Is it up to date on the field or topic?
	(Your Answer)
RELIABILITY	The preceding three questions lead to this final one: can you trust the source you have found? Does the author know what they are talking about? Is the author an expert? Has the source been vetted? Is the source *accurate, objective,* and *current*?
	(Your Answer)

Translating Incantations: Reading for Meaning

Having found some sources for your project, what comes next? Reading them of course! (NOTE: if you come across what appear to be Latin incantations, it is strongly recommended that you *not* read them out loud.)

Reading is good, but understanding is even better. The problem is that not all texts are easily digestible. Sometimes complicated ideas are hard to follow, and not all authors are equally adept at packaging information in straightforward ways. And, I hate to say this, but sometimes you need to read something more than once to fully appreciate an author's point. As with any skill, reading for meaning is one that develops over time through practice. The more you research and read, the better you get at discerning arguments and support.

This is a convenient moment to introduce the idea of rhetoric, which I discuss much more fully in Chapter Four. **Rhetoric**, put simply, is language that seeks to persuade—and my argument to you is that everything you read on some level is trying to persuade you to think, feel, believe, or act in a certain way. The two big questions then when considering sources are:

1. *What* is this piece trying to persuade me to think, feel, believe, or do?
2. And *how* does it try to get from point A to point B—that is, how does it seek to accomplish this goal?

While, as noted, we'll come back to this in Chapter Four, here are some questions you can ask of your sources while researching to help get the gist of what is going on—and, as I suggest below, this process is facilitated by taking notes as you go along.

Finding, Evaluating, and Incorporating Sources

QUESTIONS TO ASK

PURPOSE	What is the author's overall purpose? What do they want me to think, feel, or believe when I am done?
	(Your Answer)
AUDIENCE	Who is the intended audience and what assumptions does the author make about the audience's background or beliefs? Am I part of the intended audience?
	(Your Answer)
ARGUMENT, MAIN IDEAS, KEY MOMENTS	What is the author's main argument, and how does the author try to support it? What kinds of support (evidence) are introduced? What are the main points or ideas introduced to support the thesis? What are the key moments in text?
	(Your Answer)
SUCCESS	Am I persuaded by the author's argument? Why or why not? Where is the argument strongest and weakest?
	(Your Answer)

Not the Same Old Cabin in the Woods

Christina Hayward

Drew Goddard's 2012 film, *The Cabin in the Woods*, is a critique of the horror genre and its various tropes. It criticizes directors, clichés, and even the audience's own behavior and desires. By using many familiar ideas from horror films, *The Cabin in the Woods* masterfully forces audience members to think about their own desires and behaviors, how the horror film industry reuses tropes, and how they have an impact on the growth and direction of films.

The first well-known set of tropes that stuck out to me are the titles for each character. The Jock, The Whore, The Scholar, The Virgin, and The Fool are all very well-known stereotypes in horror movies. This sets certain expectations for the movie. Those familiar with slasher films expect that the promiscuous teen will be the first to be killed, swiftly followed by the jock character. *The Cabin in the Woods* begins following this pattern, only strengthening the audience's expectations. The movie takes a sharp turn when the jock character is killed by slamming into a forcefield, not by a creature. This moment is shocking and completely shatters audience expectation.

The fact that the audience is so familiar with these stereotypes and the timing of each character's death says a lot about the horror movie industry. We are so used to consuming the same carbon-copy plot with a fresh coat of paint on it. Many horror movies follow the same basic outline, but with a different monster and different character names. *The Cabin in the Woods* uses audience expectation and shock to force us to think about this normal structure and just how boring it is after seeing it done so many times.

In the movie, people need to be sacrificed in a certain pattern to appease the gods. I quickly noticed that we, the audience watching this movie, can be considered the gods. Filmmakers fit characters into stereotypes and follow the formula because it is successful and it earns them money. In a way, it appeases us. We are the reason we keep seeing the same movie over and over again. The audience has shown that it likes watching the same characters die at the hands of slightly different monsters. The audience has shown that it is okay with these tropes and has accepted that the outcome will almost always be the same. The audience has accepted predictability, but it doesn't have to be this way. We have the power to shape the film industry. We have the power to ask for something more. We have the power to say "this isn't good enough for us."

The horror movie industry has reused the same tropes for years. As an audience, we've grown to accept this pattern of characters and plot. *The Cabin in the Woods* stands as a challenge to filmmakers. It's a challenge to make something new and unique and to break away from the normal horror movie conventions. It is also a call to action for audience members. We deserve to see something innovative and to be entertained. Why pay so much money to see the same movies over and over? *The Cabin in the Woods* is both a love letter to horror and a declaration of war on the conventional horror stereotypes.

Speak Spirit! Incorporating Sources

So, you've found some useful and reliable sources for your project. How do you incorporate them into your writing?

- Step 1 is to take notes. (Sorry, but yeah—lots of work.)

The more sources you've collected, the harder it is to keep them straight—which is why note-taking becomes extremely important.

If you have personal copies that you can mark up of some or all of your sources, then you can underline or highlight, make notes in the margin, circle key words, and so on while you are reading (this is called *active reading*) and take notes when you are done.

> science fiction is a sub-category
> my examples, we will freely move between what is called horror and what is called science fiction, regarding the boundary between these putative genres as quite fluid.
>
> I plan to analyze horror as a genre. However, it should not be assumed that all genres can be analyzed in the same way. Westerns, for example, are identified primarily by virtue of their setting. Novels, films, plays, paintings, and other works, that are grouped under the label "horror" are identified according to a different sort of criteria. Like suspense novels or mystery novels, novels are denominated horrific in respect of their intended capacity to raise a certain *affect*. Indeed, the genres of suspense, mystery, and horror derive their very names from the affects they are intended to promote—a sense of suspense, a sense of mystery, and a sense of horror. The cross-art, cross-media genre of horror takes its title from the emotion it characteristically or rather ideally promotes; this emotion constitutes the identifying

Active reading defaces your text to highlight important points and vocabulary.[2]

If you are working with electronic documents or library materials, you'll need to take notes as you go along.

---

2   This passage comes from Noël Carroll's *The Philosophy of Horror, or Paradoxes of the Heart*, Routledge, 1990, p. 14.

There is no right or wrong way to do this, although there are better and worse ways. Some people still go old school with index cards, with one or more cards per source that record key phrases, figures, ideas, and terminology—make sure to record the page number or other position marker so you can find them again later!

Another option is to have a computer document where you record your thoughts and write out important passages, figures, and so on.

In both cases, bear in mind as well that what makes sense to you as you are taking notes needs to make sense to you later on when you are working on the project, so it is important to be clear.

- Step 2 is to review your notes and decide what goes where. Do this together with *outlining* (see next chapter).
- Step 3 is to incorporate your sources into your research. There are three ways to do this: *summary, paraphrase,* and *direct quotation.*

Summary: to summarize something is to state its main ideas or points concisely. Summaries are much shorter than what they are summarizing and don't bother with unnecessary details. Summary also involves putting ideas into your own words. If you are using language taken from a source, then you need to use quotation marks.

For example, consider the following passage and its summary:

The creation of Wes Craven, Freddy Krueger is the recurring antagonist of the "Nightmare on Elm Street" franchise and is a being who inhabits a dream world in which he is capable of physically murdering children while they sleep. Krueger's distinctive look is introduced in Craven's *A Nightmare on Elm Street* (1984): he wears an old hat and a red and green striped jumper, is horrifically burnt and scarred, and kills with a glove that has razor sharp claws on each finger. It is revealed that, while still alive, he was believed to have murdered over twenty children, but his trial was thrown out of court due to a legal technicality. The children Krueger preys on in the film are those of the parents who formed a mob and burnt him alive. Much of Krueger's menace is linked to our vulnerability while sleeping and he uses memories and phobias to torment his prey. Played with great relish by actor Robert Englund (b. 1947), the character is infused with a sense of mischievous fun and his crimes are fiendishly inventive, perhaps explaining why such a seemingly unsympathetic character went on to build a huge international fan base.[3]

Summary: Burned alive by an angry mob for crimes against children, Freddie Krueger is a monster who haunts nightmares in the *Nightmare on Elm Street* films. Played by actor Robert Englund, he appears horribly burnt and is marked in particular by his glove with razors. His appeal may have to do with a sense of humor and imaginative crimes (McWilliam 366–67).

Paraphrasing takes a passage from a source and puts it into your own words. Paraphrasing may condense the original somewhat, but is more detailed than a summary.

According to the poet Hesiod in his *Theogony* (c. 700 BCE), the "baneful" Hydra was the offspring of the monsters Echidna and Typhoeus, making her the sibling of Cerberus and the Chimera. The goddess Hera, who bore

---

3   David McWilliam, "Krueger, Freddy," *The Ashgate Encyclopedia of Literary and Cinematic Monsters*, edited by Jeffrey Andrew Weinstock, Ashgate, 2014, pp. 366–67.

a longstanding grudge against Heracles, nourished the Hydra herself, intending the creature as a future threat to the hero.[4]

Paraphrase: In Hesiod's *Theogony* (published around 700 BCE), the Hydra is introduced as the child of Echidna and Typhoeus, and a sibling of Cerberus and the Chimera. Hera cared for the monster herself as part of her plan to avenge herself against Heracles.

Quotation reproduces language from a source exactly as it appears in the original (and it is important that it is *exact*), and puts the quoted material in quotation marks.

A quotation from the paragraph above on the Hydra would look like this:

"The goddess Hera, who bore a longstanding grudge against Heracles, nourished the Hydra herself, intending the creature as a future threat to the hero" (Felton 338).

---

4   D. Felton, "Hydra," *The Ashgate Encyclopedia of Literary and Cinematic Monsters*, edited by Jeffrey Andrew Weinstock, Ashgate, 2014, p. 338.

So how do you know whether to summarize, paraphrase, or quote directly?

In general, it is best to quote sparingly. *Too many direct quotations in your writing has the effect of diminishing your own voice.* In situations where the author's exact wording isn't needed, it is better to paraphrase. And if all the details aren't essential, it is better to summarize.

Quote only when the author's language is particularly important. This includes:

- When the author introduces a term they have coined or that is unfamiliar to most people

  > As explained by Bosky, "Cryptids" are "organisms (plant, animal, or fungi) whose existence is suspected by some but not yet proven to the scientific community."[5]

- To show that someone indeed has made a particular claim. The example below makes clear that Young has made an assertion about the Chupacabra.

  > According to Young, "Some have speculated that the Chupacabra is extraterrestrial in origin, the product of a failed genetic experiment ..., or even a descendant of dinosaurs."[6]

---

5   Bernadette Bosky, "Cryptid," *The Ashgate Encyclopedia of Literary and Cinematic Monsters*, edited by Jeffrey Andrew Weinstock, Ashgate, 2014, p. 105.

6   Stephenie Young, "Chupacabra," *The Ashgate Encyclopedia of Literary and Cinematic Monsters*, edited by Jeffrey Andrew Weinstock, Ashgate, 2014, pp. 95–96.

- When the author says something in a particularly striking way

  Weinstock observes in his chapter on American ghosts that "Terror inevitably reflects *terroir.*"[7]

- When you want to analyze how an author says something

  A good example of H.P. Lovecraft's "purple prose" can be found in his story "The Call of Cthulhu" when he writes of the famous monster that "the Thing cannot be described—there is no language for such abysms of shrieking and immemorial lunacy, such eldritch contradictions of all matter, force, and cosmic order."[8]

YOUR TURN: SUMMARY

1. Summarize the following passage on the "Wraith" by Justin T. Noetzel. It appears in the *Ashgate Encyclopedia of Literary and Cinematic Monsters* edited by Jeffrey Weinstock. The passage below appears on page 616.

The wraith is a supernatural creature of Scottish origin that appears in literature and cinema in three different forms. It is first and foremost the ghost of a person. Secondarily, it is the immaterial

---

7   Jeffrey Andrew Weinstock, "American Ghosts," *The Routledge Handbook to the Ghost Story*, edited by Scott Brewster and Luke Thurston, Routledge, 2017, p. 206.

8   H.P. Lovecraft, "The Call of Cthulhu," *The Call of Cthulhu and Other Dark Tales*, edited by Jeffrey Andrew Weinstock, Barnes & Noble, 2009, p. 78.

or spectral projection of a living person—a "fetch" or spiritual being that is connected to an individual's soul. This second denotation frequently portends death and appears as a warning to that individual or those close to him or her. The third and least common understanding of the wraith is as an anonymous spectral figure that haunts water or the sea and often speaks or calls to those who are fated to die. The etymology of wraith is obscure, but Tom Shippey traces the word back through its Scottish origin and connects it to the Old English verb "wriðan" (to writhe) (149), an etymological connection that links wraith with "wreath" (something twisted or bent) and "wrath" (a twisted emotion and expression of anger).

2. Now paraphrase the passage. As part of your paragraph, include one direct quotation.

How to Avoid Angering the Dead

There are many scary things referenced in this guide, but the scariest of all may well be the specter of **plagiarism**. To plagiarize is to present the *words or ideas* of someone else as though they are your own. It's a form of theft, and can result in severe consequences for students and researchers (that go beyond loss of buffet privileges).

Whenever you are summarizing, paraphrasing, or quoting directly, in order to avoid provoking the spirits (and your instructor) by committing plagiarism, it is essential to be clear about the source of your ideas and language. *This must be done both in the body of the text itself and then in a separate list of references or a works cited list.*

While there are different methods of citing sources, which will be discussed in Chapter Six, the two essential steps are (1) in the body of the text, to acknowledge material that has been imported from another source and (2) to then provide a complete citation in a list of works cited (also known as references or a bibliography).

When summarizing or paraphrasing, identify the source in the body of the text. Do this by mentioning the author's name. If a source has no identifiable author, refer to it the same way it will be listed in your works cited. What is important here is that an entry in the references or works cited should unambiguously correspond to the source referenced in the text.

Note how the author is identified in the following summary:

In her article on writer George Langelaan's famous story "The Fly" and its many adaptations, Debbie Felton observes that despite the tale's scientific inaccuracies, its theme of scientific hubris remains compelling (238).

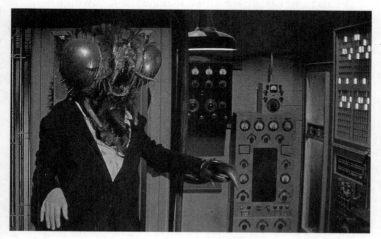

Plagiarism doesn't "fly."

This summary makes clear that the author is Debbie Felton, and that the material being summarized appears on page 238. The reader should then be able to look to a list of works cited at the end and find a complete citation for this article by Debbie Felton:

Felton, Debbie. "The Fly." *The Ashgate Encyclopedia of Literary and Cinematic Monsters*, edited by Jeffrey Andrew Weinstock, Ashgate Publishing Company, 2014, pp. 236–38.

Quoting directly comes with a few additional wrinkles.

1. In general, quotations should be prefaced (or in some cases followed) by **signal phrases**.

Signal phrases can be a few words or even a sentence; they let the reader know that you are about to incorporate a quotation. They generally mention the source's name, and sometimes provide the source's credentials or give context.

Verbs in signal phrases often include the following:

Acknowledges	Connects	Mentions
Addresses	Contends	Notes
Adds	Declares	Observes
Admits	Demonstrates	Points out
Affirms	Describes	Proposes
Alludes	Disputes	Questions
Argues	Emphasizes	Reasons
Attests	Explains	Refutes
Believes	Grants	Rejects
Claims	Highlights	Reports
Comments	Illustrates	Responds
Compares	Implies	Reveals
Confirms	Insists	Says

Shows	States	Thinks
Specifies	Suggests	Writes

Here are three examples of the use of signal phrases:

- **Regina Hansen observes that** "monstrous angels appear throughout literature and film, often inspired by religious books and treatises" (12).
- **Hansen notes that** the work of John Milton "may be the first to portray fallen angels sympathetically" (12).
- In modern fiction and film, "angels who are conventionally seen as 'good' may behave monstrously, often out of pride or impatience with human frailty" (13), **Hansen adds**.[9]

2. Put quoted material in quotation marks. In North American English, double quotation marks are used like this:

---

9   These quotations come from Regina Hansen, "Angel," *The Ashgate Encyclopedia of Literary and Cinematic Monsters*, edited by Jeffrey Andrew Weinstock, Ashgate, 2014, pp. 10–14.

The 2014 film *The Babadook* features a cheerful poem that begins, "If it's in a word, or it's in a look, you can't get rid of the Babadook."

Single quotation marks are reserved in North American English only to indicate a quotation within quotation. You are likely to encounter this most often with titles of secondary sources addressing short stories such as Daniel G. Hoffman's essay, "Irving's Use of American Folklore in 'The Legend of Sleepy Hollow.'" Note that in North American English, periods always go inside *all* quotation marks.

Apart from this relatively uncommon situation, North American English has no use for single quotation marks. The British system is the inverse—single quotation marks to signal quoted material, double quotation marks to indicate a quotation within quotation.

Remember as well that, in the North American system, periods and commas appear between quotation marks rather than after: "quoted material." (The British system is again the inverse. This has been done primarily to create confusion.)

The exception to punctuation placement with quotations is when you are citing a page number. In this case, periods are shifted such that they follow the parenthetical page notation like this:

Carol Clover writes in her study of gender and the horror film, *Men, Women, and Chain Saws*, that "the image of the distressed female most likely to linger in memory is the image of the one who did not die: the survivor, or Final Girl" (35).

Note in the example above how *no punctuation at all* appears following "Girl"—it has been shifted to follow the page number.

Wrong: "the survivor, or Final Girl." (35)
Wrong: "the survivor, or Final Girl," (35).
Wrong: "the survivor, or Final Girl"(35).
Wrong: "the survivor, or Final Girl" (page 35)

Right: **"the survivor, or Final Girl" (35).**

The final girl survives because she always cites her sources clearly and correctly, which is why she lives to fight another day.

If your quotation ends with a question mark or exclamation mark, retain that punctuation as part of the quotation, and keep everything else the same:

In his famous essay, "Monster Culture (Seven Theses)," author Jeffrey Jerome Cohen replies to the question of whether monsters actually exist with another question: "Surely they must, for if they did not, how could we?" (20).

3. Cite the source properly in the body of the text using the chosen citational format (see Chapter Six).
4. Explain the quotation.

Step #4 is an important step, but one often skipped by less experienced writers. Imagine yourself for a moment as a prosecuting attorney making a case before a jury. In order to convict the accused, *evidence* must be presented—but an experienced attorney doesn't just point to the evidence and leave it up to the jury to decide how to interpret it; instead, a good attorney explains what the evidence is, what it means, and why it is significant.

In academic writing, quotations from primary and secondary sources often serve as your "evidence" to support the claims you are making. It therefore is vital for you to explain to your reader what the quotation means and why it is important. Don't leave it up to your reader to draw their own conclusions; tell the reader what the quotation means!

For example:

> In "Monster Culture (Seven Theses)," Cohen proposes that "the monstrous body is pure culture" (4). Cohen is saying here that monsters reflect the anxieties and desires of the cultures that create them.

Learning how to find and evaluate sources is a skill developed over time through practice. As you set off to "dig up" sources, remember ye these tips of three:

1. Leave yourself enough time. I know this is easier said than done, but shoddy research is often the consequence of waiting until the last minute.
2. Give credit where credit is due, by which I mean always cite your sources. There is no swifter path to academic

perdition than to steal someone else's words or ideas and to present them as your own (and Slender Man goes after plagiarists first!).
3. Make use of the resources available to you: your instructor and librarians are there to assist you!

(Choose your own adventure Answer No. 1)

YES, TOTALLY KIDDING.

(HOWEVER, YOU CAN STILL SEND ME THE CHECK.)

CHAPTER 3

READYING THE LAB

(Brainstorming, Formulating an Argument, Outlining)

SO, YOU'VE GOT YOUR TOPIC AND, WHERE APPROPRIATE, have identified useful primary and secondary sources. What's next?

IT'S TIME TO PLAN YOUR EXPERIMENT!

This chapter will cover two important steps that often get overlooked—brainstorming and outlining—and will give some consideration to formulating arguments.

Brainstorming

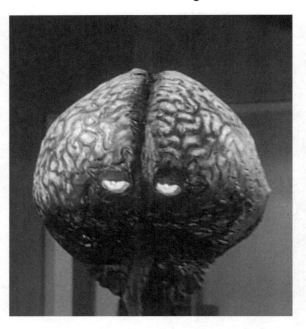

Portrait of the author while brainstorming.

Sometimes the clouds part, a beam of light shines down on you and, in a burst of inspiration, you come up with your specific topic for a paper. More commonly, one sits quietly, anxiously, torturously at one's desk mocked by the blank computer screen and trying to come up with an idea.

Often, it is more effective to go from the general to the specific rather than trying to come up all at once with a specific, polished idea. Here are some approaches to help you get going.

This activity can be performed with paper and pen, pencil, cake icing, marker, finger paint, or blood; it may also be done with a computer document (although probably not with a computer document and cake icing or blood).

1. Start with a clean page/document/notebook/scroll. Also snacks. Snacks are important here. You've heard of brain food, right?
2. *If you need to come up with a topic*: think in terms of the parameters of the assignment and generate a list of general topics you feel you could reasonably address. Write down everything that comes to mind. (If you already have a topic assigned or in mind, skip to step 4.)
3. Assuming you've come up with a range of topics, pick three that appeal to you the most or seem to have the most promise.
4. Now, have a clean page/document/notebook/scroll for each topic and engage in a process of free association. That is, write down everything you associate with that topic. This can include terms and concepts, examples, things you like or hate about it, and so on.
5. Engage in a process of *clustering*. Taking each topic, look for connections among the terms, concepts, examples, and so on. Circle ideas that seem connected and draw lines connecting them. Consider if there are other related terms that you've left out and add them. Stand back and survey your document proudly. Consider getting it framed.
6. Move from clustering to **questioning**. What we are after is an *enabling* question—a question that can lead

toward a preliminary hypothesis or thesis. Look at your clusters—what stands out about them? Why have you connected them in the way that you have? Think in terms of who/what/when/where/why/how?

Here's an example. Let's say you are being asked to develop a research paper around a particular monster and you decide to focus on vampires. Your brainstorming might look something like this (particularly if you have kids whose crayons you can steal for this activity):

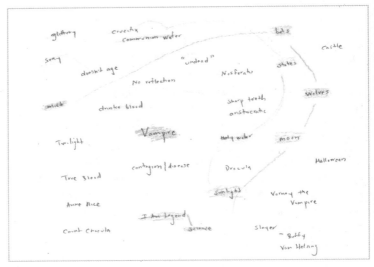

Having written down everything that comes to mind about vampires, what I then notice are several clusters of ideas:

1. Characteristics: drink blood, sharp teeth, no reflection, aristocratic, sexy, glittery, etc.
2. Ways to kill them/ward them off: sunlight, religious icons, stakes

3. Connections to animals/nature: bats, wolves, mist, moon, sun
4. Older and newer texts: *Dracula, Varney the Vampire, Nosferatu, Buffy, True Blood,* Anne Rice, *I Am Legend*
5. Vampires in popular culture: Halloween, Count Chocula

The individual terms and clusters then suggest a number of enabling questions that could form the basis for a research, argumentative, or other sort of essay:

1. How have the appearance and characteristics associated with the vampire shifted over time? Why have they changed?
2. The vampire can be killed/warded off by religious icons (holy water, crucifix, communion wafer). What is the vampire's relation to religion? Has it changed over time? If so, why?
3. Why is the vampire so immediately connected with animals (wolves, bats, rats) and the natural world? Are vampires natural predators like wolves or "supernatural"?
4. What roles do vampires play in contemporary popular culture, and why are they so consistently represented as sexy?

Here for an Argument

Academic writing frequently operates in an argumentative mode. That is, it makes a claim and then attempts to persuade the reader to accept that claim by presenting evidence in support of it. For argumentative writing, after you've narrowed your topic down and formulated questions—and, depending on the type of assignment, started to research the topic—the next step is to draft a preliminary **thesis**.

Your thesis is the main claim you are making or the position you are taking—put differently, it's the argument you are trying to win with your reader. For example, working from our brainstorming exercise above and the question about why vampires are so prominent in twenty-first-century media, we could propose a preliminary thesis along these lines: *The prominence of vampires in popular culture reflects anxiety about the waning of conventional religious observance.*

Such an essay would then go on to explore the relationship between vampires and religion in primary texts, such as novels and films, and to consider what the available secondary literature (non-fiction studies) has to say about the subject.

Picking an Argument

Here are some guidelines for coming up with thesis statements:

1. A general rule of thumb: look for something halfway between the obvious and the ridiculous.

If your argument is obvious to anyone with basic knowledge of the topic, then it isn't an argument but rather an observation. That vampires suck blood is a fact not an argument—no one could possibly argue against it. So, unless you have something more to say on the subject that goes beyond the obvious, this isn't a thesis that is going work for you.

Also avoid the "there are similarities and differences" trap. That there will be points of comparison and contrast between any two items in the same category pretty much goes without saying. Anyone who has, for example, read both Bram Stoker's *Dracula* and Stephenie Meyer's *Twilight* will know that there are similarities and differences.

So rather than saying that there are similarities and differences and leaving it at that, consider focusing instead on specific similarities and differences and developing an argument about why *they are important or worth noticing* (see point 3 below).

In contrast, if rather than being obvious your argument is ridiculous, then you can't support it. You aren't going to find any convincing evidence that Dracula in Bram Stoker's novel comes from outer space or that Stoker is actually the author of *Twilight*. This seems pretty obvious. But there are two other categories of unsupportable arguments to watch out for:

- First, *avoid arguments that derive large generalizations from limited data.* Close attention to gender roles in Stoker's *Dracula* tells us about how gender is represented in Stoker's *Dracula* (and it is pretty wild stuff!). But looking closely at one book by one author doesn't tell us anything about Victorian culture as a whole. So, if you wanted to make a larger argument about how *Dracula* reflects Victorian anxieties about gender, you'd have to consult secondary sources to help develop that.

- Second, *avoid arguing about how something would be if it were something else.* You just can't say what *Dracula* would be like if it were written by a woman, or what *Twilight* would be like if the vampire Edward was a cocker spaniel. There is no *evidence* you can introduce to substantiate your claims. All you can do is offer groundless speculation, which is never particularly convincing.

What you are therefore looking for with a thesis is something not immediately obvious, but that can be supported.

2. Second, make your thesis a statement of your argument, not what you will "explore," "consider," "address," "look into," and so on.

Sometimes when students really don't quite know yet what they are going to argue, they waffle in the introduction and phrase things in terms of a general question or topic they will "explore" or "consider" or "look into." For example, "This essay will explore the transformation of the vampire from villain in *Dracula* to hero in *Twilight*." OK, great. But that's a general topic, not a thesis.

What your reader (and instructor) wants to know is: What will your essay conclude about what's behind this transformation or what is most significant about it? Put differently, *what argument is being made?*

3. Third, avoid arguments based on personal taste.

You may think that zombies are more interesting than werewolves. Someone else may disagree. There is no way to resolve the matter since it all comes down to personal preference rather than to any kind of objective analysis of data.

With this in mind, arguments that rely on very subjective appraisals such as that one thing is "better" or "worse" than another tend not to be convincing unless very specific criteria for evaluation are introduced. Even then, readers are often left wondering why your conclusion matters. So what?

4. Fourth—and bringing together much of the above—*be specific.*

A strong thesis presents a focused argument, and lets the reader know what the argument is that the essay will develop.

See if you can mentally preface your thesis with the following words: "In this essay, I will argue *that* ..."

If you've got a *that* and it is a specific *that*, then you are headed in the right direction. If you can't complete the phrase, or you are forced to complete it with something so general that no one could possibly disagree, then it is time for some focusing.

USE OF THE FIRST AND SECOND PERSON IN ACADEMIC WRITING

As noted in Chapter One when addressing number of paragraphs, students are often taught rigid rules of writing, which include the idea that they should never use the first-person pronoun "I" in their writing. Again, you are mad—mad, I say!—and mad scientists don't play by the rules. While some instructors may still prefer that you not use the personal "I" (or, occasionally, "we" if you are working with others) in your writing, in many cases using the first person helps with clarity and is more honest. If the argument is yours, I see no reason not to claim it as such: "In this essay, I will argue...." That said, always defer to your instructor's wishes on this point.

The second person "you" however should be avoided in academic writing.

YOUR TURN

Evaluate the following thesis statements as strong or weak. If a thesis is weak, see if you can strengthen it.

1. Ogres are a type of monster.
2. Contemporary zombie films express modern anxieties about viruses and the possibility of global pandemics.
3. Andrés Muschietti's 2017 adaptation of Stephen King's novel *It* wasn't as scary as it could have been.
4. Horror films have treated women badly.
5. Jordan Peele's 2017 film *Get Out* is an allegory of American slavery.
6. Vampires are more interesting than werewolves.
7. No one should ever read or watch the *Twilight* books and films.
8. Stories about reanimated mummies convey Western guilt over the ransacking of Egyptian burial sites.

Now see if you can generate two thesis statements of your own that could serve as the organizing claim for a future paper. These may be about monsters, scary films, and mad scientists, or, if your instructor doesn't object, other topics of interest to you. The goal is to come up with the *type* of claim for which one could find appropriate support.

Outlining

I know what you are thinking: Now we're getting to the good stuff! Apart from grammatical exercises, few things are as scintillating as

outlining! Again my smart and good-looking friend, we are on the same page. A well-constructed outline is an under-appreciated thing of beauty.

Here's the thing though: some less smart and less good-looking people skip this step and just start writing willy-nilly. That's right: *I said willy-nilly*. And they do this at their peril.

Perhaps this is because they like to push the envelope, to live life on the edge. Carpe essay! Mostly though it's because they are (1) impatient to get going and (2) have waited until the last minute to start the assignment (nothing you would ever do, of course).

It is true that outlining adds an extra step to the process. However, outlining is like getting all the ingredients out you are going to need for your salsa recipe in advance: it streamlines the process and makes sure you don't omit anything. Indeed, a detailed outline can serve as the map to the essay you are about to write, and while it takes an extra few minutes to plot your course, you are likely to get to your destination a lot more quickly and with less hassle than if you just start hiking into the dark woods without really knowing where you are heading.

In the section below, I'll provide some of the standard guidelines for outlining, but an outline you make for your own use need not be formal. Any outline is better than none, and the more detailed it is, the more effectively it will guide your construction of the essay.

Here is the main thing about an outline, particularly for a thesis-driven essay: *it should make clear the logic behind the essay's organization.* That is, your points should be ordered in such a way that later points build on earlier points toward your conclusion. This then is the question you seek to answer in creating your outline: what's the most logical way to organize your points?

I suggest the following process:

1. Start by writing out your thesis: "In this essay, I will argue that ..."
2. Create a list of main points to be introduced to develop the thesis.
3. Organize those points in a way that makes sense. This may be chronological, in terms of cause and effect, classificatory, and so on.
4. Flesh out the main points: How will you develop each one? What sub-points and sources will be introduced?
5. Tweak as needed to improve logic and flow.

The most common type of outline is what is called an *alphanumeric* one—which means that it combines letters and numbers, typically in this order, as each "level" of the outline becomes more specific:

- Roman numerals (I, II, III, IV, and so on)
- Capitalized Letters (A, B, C)
- Arabic Numerals (1, 2, 3)
- Lowercase letters (a, b, c)

A generic outline therefore might look like this:

THESIS

    I. Main point 1
      A. Subheader 1
        1. Division 1
            a. Subdivision 1
            b. Subdivision 2
        2. Division 2
        3. Division 3
      B. Subheader 2
      C. Subheader 3
    II. Main point 2
    III. Main point 3
      A. Subheader 1
        1. Division 1
        2. Division 2
            a. Subdivision 1
            b. Subdivision 2
            c. Subdivision 3
      B. Subheader 2
        1. Division 1
        2. Division 2

Well-constructed outlines are exercises in logical thinking governed by four rules:

1. Coordination: Points on each "level" should have the same relative significance. So, all main points should have the same importance, all subheaders should have the same relative significance and so on.

2. Subordination: Individual sections should get progressively more specific. Main points will be the most general, subheaders more specific, divisions still more specific.
3. Parallelism: Headings, subheadings, divisions, and subdivisions should have parallel structures. For example, if the first subheader is a noun, then the rest of the subheaders should be nouns.
4. Division: Each "level" needs to have two or more parts. If there is a I then there should be a II, if you've got an A then you need at least a B, and so on.

Here is an example of a student outline for a project exploring contemporary representations of Krampus, the Christmas counterpart to Santa who punishes naughty children in European folklore.

Thesis: Contemporary representations of Krampus use him to rebuke American consumerism.

    I. Background into Krampus
        A. Connection to Saint Nicholas
        B. Terrifying appearance
        C. Role as punisher of naughty children
    II. Modern Representations
        A. *Krampus* (film)
            1. Black Friday consumer chaos
            2. Selfish dysfunctional family
            3. Krampus's killer toys
            4. Chastened family
        B. *Family Guy*
            1. Greedy child
            2. Krampus's kidnapping of child

        3. *Beauty and the Beast* allusions
        4. Realization that Krampus is misunderstood
           a. Punishes to improve
           b. Not a bad guy
III. Conclusion
    A. Krampus used to rebuke American consumerism
    B. Krampus as reminder that Christmas is about more than gifts
    C. Krampus as suggesting disciplining children important to developing character

Krampus is fun at parties!

(Choose your own adventure Answer No. 2)

A WISE GUY, HUH?

CHAPTER 4

CONDUCTING EXPERIMENTS

(Writing to Inform, Writing to Persuade, and Writing to Evaluate)

YES, TONS OF PREP WORK GOES INTO ANY DECENT EXPER-
iment. But you've gathered sources, brainstormed, outlined, and composed your preliminary thesis. (Plus, you have *not* eaten grandma, which is always a bonus.)

So, fellow mad scientists, are you ready to blow up the lab?

LET'S DO IT!

This chapter will first address tailoring your writing to suit the situation; it will then focus on three primary objectives of student writing that organize different types of assignments: Writing to Inform, Writing to Persuade, and Writing to Evaluate.

Rhetoric of the Damned: The Art of Persuasion

Simply put, *rhetoric is language that seeks to persuade.*

And the important thing is that, on some level, just about everyone you read is attempting to convince you of something.

What is the persuasive goal in each of these examples?

- No time to explain—just get in the van!
- I know it sounds crazy, but Martha is a vampire.
- Dude, get over it and meet me at 9! Everyone else will be there.
- Ogres in literature are marked by their violent tendencies and insatiable appetite.

The point is that if you are writing to someone else, you are doing so because you want them to understand something, to appreciate something, to do something, to feel something—to respond in some way—all of which involves persuasion.

What we are really talking about here, therefore, is using language to achieve your objectives (aka *manipulation*). Are you a person who likes to use language to achieve your objectives? Thought so.

So how do you use language to win friends and influence people?

Let's start with what we may refer to as *rhetorical dexterity*—the ability to alter your style to suit different circumstances and audiences so as best to achieve your intended outcome. In order for your writing to be as effective as possible, you need to be aware of three things: *context*, *audience*, and *conventions*.

- **Context** refers to the situation in which you find yourself.
- **Audience** refers to the anticipated readers of your writing.
- **Conventions** refer to the expectations that go along with writing in a particular context for a particular audience.

To illustrate: imagine you are Victor Frankenstein teaching Mad Scientist 101. You've just returned the first set of exams on how to make a monster and almost immediately find two emails treading water at the surface of your perilously deep inbox. (This is a completely made-up scenario of course. Nothing like this has ever happened. Certainly not to me. Nope.)

The first reads:

> Dear Professor Frankenstein, I received back my exam today and am concerned about my grade in your class. Would it be possible for us to meet to go over the exam together, so I can have a better understanding of what I did wrong and how to improve? Sincerely, Extremely Sincere Student

The second reads:

> The grade on my exam is compleetly unfae. I studied very hard and think I desercve a better grade.

Which of the two emails do you think would be more likely to inspire a sympathetic response from you and why?

While you are no doubt a much kinder person than I am, I can tell you from experience that the first email is more likely to go over much better with Victor (and almost every instructor everywhere)—and here's why:

- The *context* here is a student writing to an instructor about a grade received in the instructor's course.
- The *audience* is the instructor—someone in a position of authority.
- The *conventions* governing this interaction dictate a more formal style and polite approach.

I asked you above to put yourself into Victor's shoes because the ability to alter one's style to suit different contexts requires a form of empathic identification. That is, you need to imagine that you are the audience, and to tailor your language and approach for that audience. This involves being aware of *diction* and *tone*.

Diction refers to word choice. Effective writing tailors diction to suit context and audience.

If you are texting your buddies, your diction will likely be *informal*—you won't worry too much about grammar and punctuation, and may use *slang* or *colloquialisms*.

- **Slang** refers to words or phrases used in a particular context or group. This will no doubt surprise you, but teenagers sometimes use words or phrases that older people don't understand—that's slang. "Burn rubber, Daddy-O" is a kitschy way to tell someone to put the pedal to the metal, I mean to floor it, I mean to depress the accelerator fully. (Slang goes quickly out of date, so any attempt to seem current in a textbook like this is doomed from the start.)
- **Colloquialisms** may include slang but aren't limited to a particular social group; a colloquialism is a common way to refer to something that most speakers of a language will understand. Describing someone impressive as "cool" is an English-language colloquialism (unless you mean that the person actually is chilly to the touch!).

Frank is a cool dude?

Informal diction isn't always the best choice. If, for example, you are applying for a job or writing an important paper for a course (or writing to your instructor to express concern about an exam grade!), *formal* diction is a better choice. Formal diction is more sophisticated and aware of grammatical conventions.

- **Informal diction**: Victor, you totally rocked that experiment!
- **Formal diction**: Congratulations, Victor, on a successful endeavor.

Tone refers to an author or speaker's attitude toward the subject matter, the audience, or both. Tone can be dismissive, serious, humble, arrogant, sarcastic, aggressive, light-hearted, and so on.

- **Angry Tone**: That Victor Frankenstein should be permitted to perform these unholy experiments is absurd. He must be stopped immediately!
- **Light-Hearted Tone**: This composition reader is delightfully amusing! I recommend it be adopted by all college courses everywhere!

Tone can often be harder to discern in written communication than in spoken communication. When you speak, voice inflection and other cues (both verbal and non-verbal) can help listeners interpret your attitude — to tell, for example, whether you are serious or joking. Written communication lacks those cues. This is why emojis have developed for electronic communication.

Formal writing doesn't make use of emoticons or emojis. It therefore is important to pay attention to tone in formal writing and how it might be misconstrued by your reader.

Back to our two emails to Victor above.

A politely worded email—including a salutation ("Dear Professor") and closing (Sincerely)—requesting assistance demonstrates awareness of context and audience. Plus, demonstrating concern and a desire to improve both connote that the student takes the situation seriously—this is someone who wants to be the best mad scientist she can be!

An aggressive email challenging the instructor's authority is more likely to elicit a knee-jerk rejection of the student's petition than a sympathetic appraisal—and something poorly constructed and proofread will likely vindicate the instructor's evaluation rather than cause them to rethink it. Put differently: a lack of awareness of the conventions associated with a given context and audience undercuts the rhetorical effectiveness of any writing.

No doubt the authors of both emails are equally concerned; the first, however, is more aware of context, audience, and conventions, and has altered their diction and tone to suit the situation with the end point in mind: doing better in the course. The second author (who I'm

Igor has anger issues.

guessing is Igor) is venting, which may feel good at the moment, but is likely to be counterproductive in the long run.

YOUR TURN: CONTEXT, AUDIENCE, AND CONVENTIONS

1. Think about the conventions of writing associated with each of the following contexts:

- A personal statement on a job application
- A text to your friend who you hope will go with you to a Halloween haunted house
- A letter to the manager of a local restaurant after you and your friends had a terrible experience

2. In each case above, what would make the writing most likely to achieve its goal? What would prevent the message from being effective at persuading its intended audience?

3. Now bearing context and audience in mind, compose the following:

- A follow-up email to a job application to be Dr. Frankenstein's assistant submitted six weeks ago. You still haven't heard anything and want to know where you stand and if you are still in the running for a job.
- A letter to the manager of a local restaurant. You and your friends had an awful experience and you'd like to get your money back.
- An email to the instructor who gave you a D on your most recent assignment. You need at least a C- in the course or you'll have to take it again.

Rhetorical Strategies

When considering how to alter one's writing to suit different situations and audiences, we have already begun to consider *rhetorical strategies*—that is, how to be successful in persuading someone of something. And here is where things get really fun!

Consideration of rhetoric goes all the way back to ancient Greece, where the philosopher Aristotle argued that there are three elements to the art of persuasion: the appeals to *ethos*, *logos*, and *pathos*:

- Ethos says "trust me, I'm a doctor." That is, **ethos** (or the "ethical appeal") attempts to persuade an audience on the basis of character or credibility. If someone is an expert on a particular subject, their opinion carries more weight (or at least should) than that of someone who doesn't know much about that topic. Similarly, if someone has a reputation for being trustworthy, open-minded, and a straight shooter, we may weigh their opinion on something more heavily than that of someone we know to be a liar or biased.

Trust me, I'm a doctor.

- Here is what the appeal to *pathos* looks like:

When pop star Sarah McLachlan comes on your television imploring you to donate to the American Society for the Prevention of Cruelty to Animals (and, as of 2019, these spots do still run on cable!) and you start openly weeping at pictures of abused animals, and she makes you believe you are a horrible person if you don't immediately contribute, you have succumbed to emotional manipulation. To appeal to **pathos** is to attempt to persuade an audience by appealing to their emotions.

- And, of course, here is what *logos* looks like:

Star Trek's *Spock is the epitome of logic.*

The appeal to **logos** is the attempt to convince an audience through logical reasoning. This can include citing facts and statistics, providing examples and analogies, and so on.

The classical appeals are general approaches to thinking about rhetoric: is someone's attempt to persuade based on their reputation? On logical argumentation? On attempting to move you emotionally? (In actual fact, persuasion is usually a mix.)

YOUR TURN: THE CLASSICAL APPEALS

Ack! You've been cornered by a vampire who is ready to drink your blood! Try to persuade the vampire not to follow through with this in three different ways. First, appeal to *pathos*, then appeal to *logos*, lastly, appeal to *ethos*.

Alternatively, perform the same exercise but instead of trying to persuade a vampire not to drink your blood, try to persuade your instructor to give you an A on your most recent assignment.

Rhetorical Devices

However, we can get even more specific when thinking about rhetorical strategies. There are many different ways language can be used to persuade. Here are a few of the more common ones.

- An **allusion** is an indirect reference to something that creates a connection for those "in the know."

For example, if I wave my hand in front of your face and say, "These are not the droids you are looking for," those who know *Star Wars* well will recognize that this is a reference to the film and I am performing the "Jedi mind trick." This is an allusion to *Star Wars*.

- An **analogy** is a comparison between two different things.

"She screamed like a banshee" or "That guy is built like Frankenstein's monster" are both analogies that compare a person to a type of monster. Thinking of types of essays as experiments is also an analogy.

- An **anecdote** is a short story, often used to illustrate a point.

So, to illustrate this idea of anecdote, let me start with a little story: I've been teaching composition courses on and off for over twenty years, but never found a composition guide that I liked. So, the last time I was teaching English 101, it occurred to me that I should just prepare my own....

This little story is an example of an anecdote. Anecdotes can be real or invented, and can be about you or someone else.

- An **assertion** is a statement or claim.

This one is straightforward ... and my saying "this one is straightforward" is an assertion—a claim made by me.

Similarly, if I say, "The tanuki is a creature from Japanese folklore known for drinking sake, for its ability to change its shape, and for a peculiar anatomical feature," then I am making an assertion. (And seriously, you should go check out the tanuki.)

- **Authority** refers to support from authoritative sources.

If an attempt at persuasion involves referring to those knowledge-able on a topic and their findings, then the attempt makes use of authority.

For example, if I'm writing an essay about the role monsters play in religious faith and quote from Timothy K. Beal's *Religion and Its Monsters*, then I am making use of authority to bolster my argument.

- **Exaggeration** and **understatement**

Exaggeration (also known as *hyperbole*) overstates something, as in "monsters are everywhere these days." Understatement, in contrast, presents something as smaller or less important than it really is, as in "yes, Godzilla did a little bit of damage to Tokyo."

- **Metaphor** and **simile**

Metaphors and similes compare unlike objects to one another. Metaphor does this directly by saying one object is another, as in "the werewolf's howl was a dagger through our hearts." In this case, the howl is being compared to a dagger.

Simile does the same thing, but uses "like" or "as": "Victor's creation was stitched together like a quilt." The comparison here is between the creation and a quilt.

YOUR TURN: RHETORICAL DEVICES

Come up with your own examples for some or all of the rhetorical devices above. They may be silly or serious, but should show an understanding of the concept.

Rhetorical Fallacies

A fallacy is something that is false. Rhetorical fallacies are errors in reasoning that undermine your argument. Often, they are claims that either lack evidence or are tangential to the point being made. There are lots of them. Here are a few of the most common:

- The **ad hominem**. This is a personal attack rather than an analysis of evidence.

While it is tempting to refer to contemporary politicians here, we'll exercise great restraint with our example. If we attempt to argue that Victor Frankenstein's project to reanimate dead flesh is flawed because Victor is a philandering drunkard, we have committed an ad hominem attack. We aren't actually arguing against his project; we're instead attacking Victor's character.

- The **bandwagon fallacy**. This encourages an audience to agree just because others agree. If everyone else jumped off a bridge, would you do it?

- The **causal fallacy**. This confuses chronology with causality. Just because B happened after A doesn't mean that A caused B.

For example, your phone rang and then it started raining. It's pretty unlikely that your phone ringing made it rain. To attribute the rain to your phone ringing would be a causal fallacy (unless you have some kind of cursed or magic phone—do you?!).

- The **circular argument**. This begins with its intended end point.

For example: Jason Voorhees is a monster because of his monstrous qualities.

- The **false dichotomy**. This argument takes a complicated issue and turns it into an either/or situation.

Example: "Either something is a monster or it isn't."

Well, no. It isn't that simple. You have to start by figuring out what you mean by monster. Is a monster someone whose appearance deviates from the norm? Or is monstrosity defined by how something acts? What if its actions are in accordance with its nature? Or if someone does horrible things as a result of mental illness? Is a terrorist a monster if you agree with the cause they stand for? And what about a werewolf—someone who is only a monster part of the time?

The point is that the assertion "either something is a monster or it isn't" presents a false dichotomy. It is an oversimplification that fails to acknowledge many other factors.

- The **hasty generalization**. This draws conclusions based on scanty or suspect evidence.

If there is one thing that horror movies teach us, it is to beware of hasty generalizations:

Having successfully combated the vampire, we can conclude that our problems with Dracula are over.

- The **moral equivalence**. This compares minor problems with much greater ones.

The term "grammar Nazi" falsely equates someone persnickety about grammar with systematic genocide.

- The **red herring**. I know, this one sounds delicious, but it isn't. A red herring is when misleading or unrelated evidence is introduced to support a conclusion.

Horror films and mysteries are often built around red herrings—clues that lead us in the wrong direction, and distract us from figuring out what is really going on or who the real monster is too soon. The problem with discussing red herrings is that they inevitably end up as spoilers. But I'll give you one example: in *Saw*, Zepp, the hospital orderly, isn't who much of the film leads us to believe he is.

- The **slippery slope**. The slippery slope argument claims without evidence that if A happens, then inevitably B, C, D, and so on will follow.

We hear this one all the time in political discourse. If same-sex marriage is legalized, next people will want to marry major appliances. Any regulation on firearms will inevitably lead to the mass confiscation of all firearms. The slippery slope fallacy is a way to create hysteria by suggesting that a relatively minor action will inevitably lead to major and even absurd results.

- The **straw man**. This is an argument that attacks a simplified position that one's opponent doesn't really hold.

I say: "Well, not all things conventionally regarded as monsters are bad."

My opponent: "You think monsters are good! You support monsters eating our children! Ladies and gentlemen, you heard it yourself. Professor Weinstock has chosen monsters over you!"

YOUR TURN: RHETORICAL FALLACIES

Devise examples of three of the rhetorical fallacies above. They may be serious or silly, monster-related or not, but should demonstrate how the fallacy works.

YOUR TURN: THE RHETORICAL ANALYSIS

Read the essay below and then analyze the way it seeks to persuade its reader. What rhetorical strategies does it utilize? Where is it most persuasive? Where is it weakest?

Monsters and the Moral Imagination[1]

Monsters are on the rise. People can't seem to get enough of vampires lately, and zombies have a new lease on life. This year and next we have the release of the usual horror films like *Saw VI* and *Halloween II*; the campy mayhem of *Zombieland*; more-pensive forays like *9* (produced by Tim Burton and Timur Bekmambetov), *The Wolfman*, and *The Twilight Saga: New Moon*; and, more playfully, *Where the Wild Things Are* (a Dave Eggers rewrite of the Maurice Sendak classic).

The reasons for this increased monster culture are hard to pin down. Maybe it's social anxiety in the post-9/11 decade, or the conflict in Iraq—some think there's an uptick in such fare during wartime. Perhaps it's the economic downturn. The monster proliferation can be explained, in part, by exploring the meaning of monsters. Popular culture is re-enchanted with meaningful monsters, and even the eggheads are stroking their chins—last month saw the seventh global conference on Monsters and the Monstrous at the University of Oxford.

The uses of monsters vary widely. In our liberal culture, we dramatize the rage of the monstrous creature—and Frankenstein's is a good example—then scold ourselves and our "intolerant society" for alienating the outcast in the first place. The liberal lesson of monsters is one of tolerance: We must overcome our innate scapegoating, our xenophobic tendencies. Of course, this is by no means the only interpretation of monster stories. The medieval mind saw giants and mythical creatures as God's punishments for the sin of pride. For the Greeks and

---

1   Stephen T. Asma, "Monsters and the Moral Imagination," *The Chronicle Review*, 25 October 2009, https://www.chronicle.com/article/Monstersthe-Moral/48886.

Romans, monsters were prodigies—warnings of impending calamity.

After Freud, monster stories were considered cathartic journeys into our unconscious—everybody contains a Mr. Hyde, and these stories give us a chance to "walk on the wild side." But in the denouement of most stories, the monster is killed and the psyche restored to civilized order. We can have our fun with the "torture porn" of Leatherface and Freddy Krueger or the erotic vampires, but this "vacation" to where the wild things are ultimately helps us return to our lives of quiet repression.

Any careful reading of Bram Stoker's *Dracula*, for example, will reveal not only a highly sexualized description of blood drinking, but an erotic characterization of the count himself. Even John Polidori's original 1819 vampire tale *The Vampyre* describes the monster as a sexually attractive force. According to the critic Christopher Craft, Gothic monster tales—*Frankenstein, The Strange Case of Dr. Jekyll and Mr. Hyde, Dracula*, Anne Rice's Vampire Chronicles—rehearse a similar story structure. "Each of these texts first invites or admits a monster, then entertains and is entertained by monstrosity for some extended duration, until in its closing pages it expels or repudiates the monster and all the disruption that he/she/it brings," he writes.

A crucial but often-ignored aspect of monsterology is the role those beasties play in our moral imaginations. Recent experimental moral psychology has given us useful tools for looking at the way people actually do their moral thinking. Brain imaging, together with hypothetical ethical dilemmas about runaway trolley cars, can teach us a lot about our real value systems and actions. But another way to get at this subterranean territory is by looking at our imaginative lives.

Monsters can stand as symbols of human vulnerability and crisis, and as such they play imaginative foils for thinking about

our own responses to menace. Part of our fascination with
serial-killer monsters is that we (and our loved ones) are poten-
tially vulnerable to sadistic violence—never mind that statistical
probability renders such an attack almost laughable. Irrational
fears are decidedly unfunny. We are vulnerable to both the
inner and the outer forces. Monster stories and films only draw
us in when we identify with the persons who are being chased,
and we tacitly ask ourselves: Would I board up the windows to
keep the zombies out or seek the open water? Would I go down
to the basement after I hear the thump, and if so, would I bring
the butcher knife or the fireplace poker? What will I do when I
am vulnerable?

The comedy writer Max Brooks understands that dimension
of monster stories very well. In books like *The Zombie Survival
Guide* and *World War Z*, Brooks gives us painstaking, haunt-
ing, and hilarious advice about how best to meet our undead
foes. For its April Fools' edition, the otherwise serious journal *Archaeology* interviewed Brooks, asking him (tongue firmly
in cheek): "Does the archaeological record hold any zombie-re-
lated lessons for us today? What can our ancestors teach us
about meeting and, ultimately, defeating the undead menace?"
Brooks replied: "The greatest lesson our ancestors have to teach
us is to remain both vigilant and unafraid. We must endeavor
to emulate the ancient Romans; calm, efficient, treating zombies
as just one more item on a rather mundane checklist. Panic is
the undead's greatest ally, doing far more damage, in some
cases, than the creatures themselves. The goal is to be prepared,
not scared, to use our heads, and cut off theirs."

Brooks is unparalleled in parodying a well-worn monster
tradition, but he wouldn't be so funny if we weren't already
using monster stories to imagine strategies for facing enemies.
The monster is a virtual sparring partner for our imagination.
How will I avoid, assuage, or defeat my enemy? Will I have

grace under pressure? Will I help others who are injured? Or will I be that guy who selfishly goes it alone and usually meets an especially painful demise?

In a significant sense, monsters are a part of our attempt to envision the good life or at least the secure life. Our ethical convictions do not spring fully grown from our heads but must be developed in the context of real and imagined challenges. In order to discover our values, we have to face trials and tribulation, and monsters help us imaginatively rehearse. Imagining how we will face an unstoppable, powerful, and inhuman threat is an illuminating exercise in hypothetical reasoning and hypothetical feeling.

You can't know for sure how you will face a headless zombie, an alien face-hugger, an approaching sea monster, or a chain-saw-wielding psycho. Fortunately, you're unlikely to be put to the test. But you might face similarly terrifying trials. You might be assaulted, be put on the front lines of some war, or be robbed, raped, or otherwise harassed and assailed. We may be lucky enough to have had no real acquaintance with such horrors, but we have all nonetheless played them out in our mind's eye. And though we can't know for sure how we'll face an enemy soldier or a rapist, it doesn't stop us from imaginatively formulating responses. We use the imagination in order to establish our own agency in chaotic and uncontrollable situations.

People frequently underestimate the role of art and imagery in their own moral convictions. Through art (e.g., Shelley's *Frankenstein*, Hitchcock's *Psycho*, King's and Kubrick's *The Shining*), artists convey moral visions. Audiences can reflect on them, reject or embrace them, take inspiration from them, and otherwise be enriched beyond the entertainment aspect. Good monster stories can transmit moral truths to us by showing us examples of dignity and depravity without preaching or proselytizing.

But imagining monsters is not just the stuff of fiction. Picture yourself in the following scenario. On the evening of August 7, 1994, Bruce Shapiro entered a coffee bar in New Haven, Conn. Shapiro and his friends had entered the cafe and were relaxing at a table near the front door. Approximately 15 other people were scattered around the bar, enjoying the evening. One of Shapiro's friends went up to the bar to get drinks. "Suddenly there was chaos," Shapiro explained in *The Nation* the next year, "as if a mortar shell had landed." He looked up to see a flash of metal and people leaping away from a thin, bearded man with a ponytail. Chairs and tables were knocked over, and Shapiro protected one of his friends by pulling her to the ground.

In a matter of minutes, the thin man, Daniel Silva, had managed to stab and seriously injure seven people in the coffee shop. Using a six-inch hunting knife, Silva jumped around the room and attacked with lightning speed. Two of Shapiro's friends were stabbed. After helping some others, Shapiro finally escaped the cafe. "I had gone no more than a few steps," he recalled, "when I felt a hard punch in my back followed instantly by the unforgettable sensation of skin and muscle tissue parting. Silva had stabbed me about six inches above my waist, just beneath my rib cage."

Shapiro fell to the pavement and cried out, "Why are you doing this?" Standing over him, Silva plunged the knife into Shapiro's chest, beneath his left shoulder. "You killed my mother" was the incoherent response that Silva offered his victim. Silva then pulled the knife out of Shapiro and rode off on a bicycle. He was soon apprehended and jailed.

Was Silva a monster? Not exactly. He was a mentally ill man who snapped and seemed to think that his mother had been wronged and felt some obscure need to avenge her. (She was, in fact, in a nearby hospital at the time, being treated for diabetes.) But from the perspective of raw experience, this horrifying event shares many qualities with the imagined monster attack. Shapiro and his unfortunate company were suddenly presented with a deadly, irrational, powerful force that sent them reeling for mere survival. And yet the victims demonstrated an impressive ability to reach out and help each other. While the victims were leaping away from Silva's angry knife blade, I suspect that he was for them, practically speaking, a true monster. I would never presume to correct them on that account. In such circumstances, many of us are sympathetic to the use of the monster epithet.

One of the fascinating aspects of Shapiro's experience is how people responded to his story after the fact. I have been suggesting that monster stories are encapsulations of the human feeling of vulnerability—the monster stories offer us the "disease" of vulnerability and its possible "cures" (in the form of heroes and coping strategies). Few monster stories remain indefinitely in the "threat phase." When fear is at a fever pitch, they always move on to the hero phase. Hercules slays the Hydra, George slays the dragon, medicine slays the alien virus, the stake and crucifix slay the vampire. Life and art mutually seek to conquer vulnerability. "Being a victim is a hard idea to accept," Shapiro explained, "even while lying in a hospital bed with tubes in veins, chest, penis, and abdomen. The spirit rebels against the idea of oneself as fundamentally powerless."

This natural rebellion may have prompted the most repeated question facing Shapiro when he got out of the hospital. When people learned of Daniel Silva's attack on seven victims, they asked, "Why didn't anyone try to stop him?" Shapiro always tried to explain how fast and confusing the attack was, but people failed to accept this. Shapiro, who was offended by the question, says, "The question carries not empathy but an implicit burden of blame; it really asks 'Why didn't *you* stop him?' It is asked because no one likes to imagine oneself a victim." We like to see ourselves as victors against every threat, but of course that's not reality.

Believers in human progress, from the Enlightenment to the present, think that monsters are disappearing. Rationality will pour its light into the dark corners and reveal the monsters to be merely chimeric. A familiar upshot of the liberal interpretation of monsters is to suggest that when we properly embrace difference, the monsters will vanish. According to this view, the monster concept is no longer useful in the modern world. If it hangs on, it does so like an appendix—useful once but hazardous now.

I disagree. The monster concept is still extremely useful, and it's a permanent player in the moral imagination because human vulnerability is permanent. The monster is a beneficial foe, helping us to virtually represent the obstacles that real life will surely send our way. As long as there are real enemies in the world, there will be useful dramatic versions of them in our heads.

In 2006, four armed men in Kandahar, Afghanistan, broke into the home of an Afghan headmaster and teacher named Malim Abdul Habib. The four men held Habib as they gathered his wife and children together, forcing them to watch as they stabbed Habib eight times and then decapitated him. Habib was the headmaster at Shaikh Mathi Baba high school, where he educated girls along with boys. The Taliban militants of the region, who are suspected in the beheading, see the education of girls as a violation of Islam (a view that is obviously not shared by the vast majority of Muslims). My point is simply this: If you can gather a man's family together at gunpoint and force them to watch as you cut off his head, then you are a monster. You don't just seem like one; you are one.

A relativist might counter by pointing out that American soldiers at Abu Ghraib tortured some innocent people, too. That, I agree, is true and astoundingly shameful, but it doesn't prove there are no real monsters. It only widens the category and recognizes monsters on both sides of an issue. Two sides calling each other monsters doesn't prove that monsters don't exist. In the case of the American torturer at Abu Ghraib and the Taliban beheader in Afghanistan, both epithets sound entirely accurate.

My own view is that the concept of monster cannot be erased from our language and thinking. It cannot be replaced by other more polite terms and concepts, because it still refers to something that has no satisfactory semantic substitute or refinement. The term's imprecision, within parameters, is part of its usefulness. Terms like "monster" and "evil" have a lot of metaphysical residue on them, left over from the Western traditions. But even if we neuter the term from obscure theological questions about Cain, or metaphysical questions about demons, the language still successfully expresses a radical frustration over the inhumanity of some enemy. The meaning of "monster" is found in its context, in its use.

So this Halloween season, let us, by all means, enjoy our fright fest, but let's not forget to take monsters seriously, too. I'll be checking under my bed, as usual. But remember, things don't strike fear in our hearts unless our hearts are already seriously committed to something (e.g., life, limb, children, ideologies, whatever). Ironically then, inhuman threats are great reminders of our own humanity. And for that we can all thank our zombies.

Experiment Time

Let's get down to business now. Academic writing typically falls into three categories: writing to inform, writing to persuade, and writing to evaluate. (All three forms actually engage in persuasion; however, writing to persuade is more explicitly focused on proving an argument.)

Channeling Information: Writing to Inform

When you write to inform, your goal is to convey information clearly to your audience. The information may be about something that happened, how to do something, what something is, and so on. To convey information clearly is a straightforward but challenging goal: it requires you to express ideas clearly and in a logical order, and to bear in mind the audience for whom you are writing.

Here is an example of a short informational essay on the Australian monster known as the Yowie:

The Yowie

The yowie, like the bunyip, originates in the mythology of Aboriginal Australians and was incorporated into colonial folklore. The yowie may also be referred to as the indigenous ape, the Hairy Man, or yahoo, and is distinguished from other native monsters by its humanoid form. It inhabits wooded or bush locales. Yowies are typically described as giant men, excessively hairy, with large feet, a talent for climbing, and a taste for eating humans—especially women. They have also been described as possessing backwards feet and red faces, although these traits are not uniform.

Tracing the history of yowie appearances by name alone is quite challenging, due to the diversity of Aboriginal linguistic and cultural groups and the difficulties colonizers experienced in communicating with the populations they encountered. White colonizers adopted the terms yowie and bunyip, but during the nineteenth century often used the terms interchangeably for any bush monster (Holden 47–48).

Prior to the twentieth century, most references to yowies or yahoos are in newspaper or magazines articles, rather than in fiction. These references include sightings, such as reported in the *Australian Town and Country Journal* on November 4, 1876 and November 18, 1876, and the *Australian and New Zealand Monthly Magazine*, which ran an article "Superstitions of the Australian Aborigines: The Yahoo" in February 1842.

Judging from the relatively few examples in Australian fiction and film, the yowie did not achieve the same dissemination within colonial folklore that its compatriot the bunyip did. There are, however, some standout examples. May Gibbs' villainous Banksia Men in *Snugglepot and Cuddlepie* (1918) are good examples of the abduction narrative common to folk stories about yowies. Inclusion in poetry has not been significant, but the yowie appears in poems by Norman Smith "Yowie" (1983) and Lynnette McKenzie "The Yowie" (1982). The beast has featured in children's picture books by Ann Ferns including *The Yowie Finds a Home* (1981), *The Yowie Is Very Brave* (1981), and *The Adventures of the Yowie* (1983); Geoff Barlow's 1995 mystery novel *The Yarra Yowie* also made use of the creature.

In 1997, Cadbury launched a range of Yowie chocolates, which were accompanied by an advertising campaign showing each colored yowie in a different Australian eco-system and encouraging children to take care of their native flora and fauna. The original concept for these yowies came from Geoff Pike, who authored a series of children's picture books on the same themes, also published in 1997. *The Midnight Monster* by Edel Wignell, published in 1998, features a young girl being stalked by a "wow-ee" (a variant spelling of yowie) during the night. *Nor of Human: An Anthology of Fantastic Creatures* (2001) edited by Geoffrey Maloney features two yowie stories. In 2010, a short film titled *The Yowie* directed by Jens Hertzum explored the difficulties of small down life, as a father (Alan Dearth) and son (Samuel Faull) manufacture yowie sightings in their local area in a bid to increase tourism.

A misunderstood yowie just trying to give a hug.

The yowie, although less popular in Australian fiction and film than other mythic creatures, remains an important element within Australia's folklore and indigenous oral histories.[2]

YOUR TURN: EXPERIMENTING WITH INFORMATION

- Write an informational essay that explains to your reader the steps involved in creating a monster or explain the best way to survive a zombie apocalypse.
- Alternatively, write an informational essay similar to the yowie example above: research and explain the characteristics and origins of a monster or other supernatural creature of your choice.

Develop your essay using the steps outlined in Chapter Three: begin with brainstorming and then move on to an outline.

---

2   From A.C. Blackmore, "Yowie," *The Ashgate Encyclopedia of Literary and Cinematic Monsters*, edited by Jeffrey Andrew Weinstock, Ashgate, 2014, pp. 619–20.

MIRRORING THE SOUL:
THE PERSONAL REFLECTION

One way to appeal to *ethos*—that is, to establish your authority to speak on a particular topic—is to introduce your own experience. The process of *reflection* often asks you to consider your personal experiences and to draw conclusions based on them. Put differently, the act of reflection involves interpretation of your history and experiences.

(Movies involving flashbacks often function in a reflective mode as a more mature narrator tells what happened to them as a kid and then explains what they couldn't appreciate at the time: how they were being shaped by their experiences.)

Reflective writing also generally has a point to it. In some cases, the reflection may confirm or refute something seen, heard, or read—that is, reflecting on your own experiences may allow you to evaluate someone else's claims. In other cases, the reflection may be part of a larger argument—a personal anecdote can lead into an argumentative essay for example.

YOUR TURN: REFLECTIVE EXPERIMENTS

1. Assume the persona of a mad scientist reflecting on an experiment that has gone awry. Explain your experiment and what you learned from it.
2. Adopt the persona of a monster. Share your experiences and what you learned from them or how they shaped you.
3. Reflect on an experience that had a profound impact on you (monster-related or not). Summarize the experience and then explain how it shaped you and/or what you learned.

Develop your essay using the steps outlined in Chapter Three: begin with brainstorming and then move on to an outline.

UNHOLY MASH-UP? SYNTHESIZING SOURCES

Some questions have simple yes/no answers. Does Godzilla smash up Tokyo? Yes. Are you both extremely intelligent and good looking? Absolutely. Is this the best composition guide ever? Of course.

However, few things in life, alas, are this simple. Most important issues have many sides to them, and to water them down to an either/or yes/no set of options results in distortion and oversimplification (see "False Dichotomy" in the rhetorical fallacies section above).

Often in academic writing, prior to weighing in on a debate, you need to offer an overview of the existing positions on a question or subject. A synthesis essay is one that explains the different positions on a topic by bringing together (synthesizing) different voices that have weighed in on it.

To do this, you need to:

- First, research the issue and identify the different critics, researchers, or commentators who have weighed in on it;
- Second, group those different voices together based on their positions; and
- Third, present those different groupings of voices in a clear and logical way.

While a synthesis component may be an important part of an argumentative essay, synthesis is different from argument. Your goal in writing a synthesis is to fairly and objectively summarize the different positions on the question or topic without taking a side.

Your thesis will likely identify the different positions on the issue.

For example, one could synthesize the different positions on Victor Frankenstein's experiment to create life out of pieces of corpses. Let's say research results in the following opinions:

- Victor's experiment was intrinsically wrong. Only God should create life. Victor's project was hubristic and arrogant.
- There was nothing intrinsically wrong with Victor's experiment, but he went about it the wrong way. He should have been above board all along, sought permission to use body parts, and subjected himself to appropriate oversight.
- Victor erred not in performing his experiments, but turning his back on his creation after he endowed it with life. The problem wasn't his experiment, but his response to it.
- Despite the dark outcome of Victor's tale, his experiment should be regarded as a complete success, and one with great potential to benefit humanity.

One could organize these positions into the following thesis statement:

Critical evaluation of Victor Frankenstein's experiments results in four main perspectives: that Victor's experiment usurped God's prerogative, that Victor's aspirations were noble but he pursued them in the wrong way, that Victor erred primarily in not taking responsibility for his creation, and that, despite the tale's dark outcome, Victor was entirely successful in what he attempted to achieve.

A thesis such as this sets up an organized informative essay (or section of an essay) that addresses each of these positions in the order introduced in the thesis with reference to the critics that articulate those positions. (Always address points in the body of the essay in the same order they are presented at the start.)

YOUR TURN: SYNTHESIS EXPERIMENTS

Research the different positions on one of the following topics, then write a thesis statement for a synthesis essay on the topic.

- In science fiction writer H.G. Wells's *The Island of Dr. Moreau*, the mad scientist Dr. Moreau creates human-animal hybrids. In the existing literature on biomedical ethics, what points of view exist concerning this and similar "real-world" practices?
- Horror films presumably seek to scare us. If being scared is unpleasant, why would anyone seek to be scared? Explore the available research on why horror films appeal to viewers and outline the main positions.
- A monster-free alternative: explore the different positions that exist on a contemporary issue with more than two sides. Such issues could include whether student athletes should be paid, gun control, stem cell research, or the healthiest diet.

If your instructor directs, then develop your essay using the steps outlined in Chapter Three: begin with brainstorming and then move on to an outline.

Here for an Argument

Thesis-driven persuasive essays are among the most common types of essays assigned in college courses. They typically take the forms of either argumentative essays built around close reading, research essays advancing a particular claim, or a combination of the two.

An argumentative essay requires you to advance a position on a topic (see discussion of thesis in Chapter Three). Such an essay is typically constructed along these lines:

1. An **introduction** that includes a thesis and explains why the topic is important
2. **Body paragraphs** that support the thesis and build on one another toward the conclusion
3. A **conclusion** that makes clear the significance of the argument

Let's take these sections one at a time.

IN THE BEGINNING ...

A well-crafted introduction actually does four things:

1. Introduces the general topic an essay will address,
2. Presents a position on that topic to be developed (the thesis),
3. Outlines how the thesis will be developed, and
4. Makes clear to the reader why they should care.

Tip: Avoid "cosmic introductions." Unless you honestly mean since the Big Bang or since the first human stood upright, avoid starting an essay of any kind with an inflated claim such as "since the dawn of time," "since the beginning of time," "since the start of human history," and so on. Broad, sweeping generalizations such as this are almost always wrong—and there is no worse way to start an essay than with a fallacious claim! (You can't convince anyone that you know what you're talking about if they think you believe dinosaurs debated ethics.)

Consider this example by undergraduate Sara Wene as part of a research essay on the story of Sweeney Todd:

First published in 1846 as a Penny Dreadful serial, *The String of Pearls* shocked many readers across Great Britain with its plot line about revenge. Like most other Penny Dreadful series of the time, *The String of Pearls* is a story full of horror, gore, and murder. Set in 1785, London, the protagonist, Sweeney Todd, is a middle-aged barber who kills his customers and takes their bodies to his friend, Mrs. Lovett, who then bakes their flesh into meat pies. The story of Sweeney Todd (later turned into a musical with the same name) touches on many social anxieties including cannibalism and fear about the food we eat. However, a central theme is also that people may not be what they appear to be on the surface. Through attention to the characters Mrs. Lovett, Judge Turpin, and Sweeney Todd himself, I will argue that duplicity and hypocrisy are central to the narrative, and that this is one reason the story continues to resonate with us today. While we hopefully will never experience cannibalism, all of us likely have encountered someone with more than one face.

PIECES OF THE BODY

As discussed in Chapter One, each body paragraph should help support the thesis and should be focused around one main idea. Support may consist of close reading and analysis of primary sources, anecdote, facts and statistics, and reference to or quotation from secondary sources.

Avoid cherry picking support: To "cherry pick" support is to ignore inconvenient data, and it is in fact a kind of rhetorical fallacy. When you only introduce evidence that supports your claim and ignore everything that doesn't, you present an incomplete picture and open yourself up to the charge of "cherry picking." The stronger the withheld data is, the weaker your argument is.

What you therefore need to do is to acknowledge that there are other positions or counter-arguments, and to explain why your conclusion is more compelling. Depending on the specifics of your argument, it may work better to dedicate a specific paragraph to this, though you can also briefly acknowledge and refute counterarguments in body paragraphs that primarily advance your own points. The trick here is to make sure that for every opposing position you acknowledge, you have a convincing reason why your position is stronger!

FINAL DESTINATION: THE CONCLUSION

While this is obvious, it is still worth stressing: your conclusion is the last thing your audience is going to read. If your reader comes away scratching their head and wondering either what your point was or why it matters, then your experiment has fallen flat. Here then are some tips for conclusive conclusions.

1. First, before you do anything, look back to your introduction and find your thesis. Is the thesis presented there what the paper actually ended up arguing? If not, some revision will be needed (likely to the introduction). See Chapter Five on revision.

2. Assuming the paper you've written argues the thesis presented at the start, your conclusion should remind the reader what the argument has been and be clear about why it matters. Your conclusion is the place to stress the implications of your argument. Put differently, if your reader gets to the end of your essay and says, "OK, so what?" your conclusion should have the answer!

3. While your conclusion can suggest possible further avenues for exploration or next steps, it isn't the place to introduce a completely new idea. Nothing should "come out of left field" in the conclusion.

YOUR TURN: ARGUMENTATIVE EXPERIMENTS

- Pick a contemporary monster of your choice and develop an argument concerning how it reflects a contemporary anxiety or desire.

- Myths and legends concerning monsters often find their roots in social practices, physiological abnormality, and religious belief. Research the background of a monster of your choice and determine how belief in such a creature could have arisen. (Remember that this is meant as an argumentative essay, so develop an assertive thesis!)

- Alternatively, pick a primary text with which you are familiar and develop a thesis concerning how that primary text reinforces or undermines a common stereotype. Your primary text can be a television program, a song, a YouTube video, a blog, and so on. Once you have developed your thesis, support it by introducing specific details from your primary text and illustrate your claim.

Develop your essay using the steps outlined in Chapter Three: begin with brainstorming and then move on to an outline.

Success or Failure? Writing to Evaluate

We engage in the process of evaluation all the time. Do you like this book? Why or why not? What did you think of the most recent entry in the *Star Wars* film series? Which restaurant near campus has the best pizza? Who is the scariest slasher movie villain—Jason, Michael, or Freddy?

And we live in a world where (for better or worse) consumers are insistently invited to evaluate products and services—Amazon.com, Yelp, Angie's List, and even end-of-the-semester student opinion surveys and evaluations all ask consumers for feedback.

Evaluative essays are ones in which authors use a set of criteria to determine the quality or effectiveness of something. What's important here—and what often sets formal evaluative essays apart from reviews on Amazon or Yelp—is to be very clear about the yardstick you are using for your assessment.

- The first step in composing an evaluative essay, then, is to brainstorm the criteria you will use to assess the quality of your subject.

With that in mind, what criteria could you use to evaluate the following?

1. A horror film
2. An amusement park
3. A guidebook on composition

It is also important in an evaluative essay to be clear about possible evaluative criteria *not* being considered. For example, should a list of criteria for evaluating the best pizza include price? Well, that depends whether you are looking just for the best-tasting pizza or the "best bang for the buck." Reviews need to be clear about these things!

- Once you have your criteria figured out, the next step is to apply those criteria in an organized and clear way to the thing being evaluated.

Evaluative essays typically are organized as follows:

1. An introduction that outlines a position and the criteria used
2. Focused body paragraphs that each apply an individual criterion and provide examples or illustrations to justify the application
3. A conclusion that reasserts the thesis in light of the evidence supplied

Here, for example, is a book review by undergraduate Jade Driscoll:

Monstrous Representations in *Monster High*

Although many people are familiar with common monsters, exact introductions to monsters come in a variety of ways. People may see monstrous characters in television shows, movies, or stories. One modern presentation of monsters for young adult readers is the book *Monster High*. Throughout the book, author Lisi Harrison portrays the sons and daughters of monsters across history. *Monster High* is a clever, modern take on monsters that introduces young adult readers to relatable creatures of the night while including elements from the classic tales. Engaging in its own right, the story also then prompts its audience to look further into its sources of inspiration.

Harrison introduces numerous monsters throughout the book, but the first one readers meet is Frankie Stein, based off Frankenstein's monster. Created by her father and implanted with fifteen years' worth of knowledge, Frankie is a high school sophomore with green skin and large bolts on her neck (Harrison 13). Every day, Frankie has to charge herself through the neck bolts to keep from powering down. However, running off electricity was not a trait of Frankenstein's monster, but an addition by Harrison.

Even though Frankie is not exactly like the original monster, her appearance allows young adult readers to connect with her more readily. She is around the same age as the target audience and deals with many of the same struggles, yet she maintains the basic traits of Frankenstein's monster. The original monster is even alluded to as being Frankie's "grandfather." Therefore, even though readers are learning about a modern-ized version of the monster, they are still able to learn about what influenced Frankie.

Another main character in Harrison's book is Draculaura, a vampire based off the famed Dracula. Draculaura shares many similarities with standard vampires; she has fangs, lacks a reflection, and is always cold. These traits are similar to original stories, but the largest difference between Draculaura and Dracula is that she does not drink blood. She hates the thought of harming animals to get blood, so she takes in protein and iron by taking supplement pills every day (Harrison 67). Refusing to drink blood is a huge difference between her and original vampires.

Just as with Frankie, the differences between Draculaura and Dracula do not stop readers from learning about the original monsters. Draculaura becomes a character that more young adults can relate to, but they get pieces of the original story. They still see that vampires usually need blood to survive, as well as the various physical descriptors listed above. Draculaura may have some huge differences from her character's inspiration, but not at the cost of leaving out all elements of the vampire.

The characters in *Monster High* deviate from their inspiration quite a bit, yet readers still learn about the original monsters. By making the characters more relatable to a young adult audience, Harrison is able to showcase standard monster stories for a new generation. Still, Harrison makes sure to include elements of the original monsters and their stories. Even with the deviations, the book still succeeds in introducing young adult readers to various monsters throughout history, inspiring them to then go on and read further.

Work Cited

Harrison, Lisi. *Monster High*. Poppy, 2010.

YOUR TURN: EVALUATIVE EXPERIMENTS

Generate evaluative criteria and prepare an evaluative essay on one of the following:

1. You. Alas, you have passed away. (Sorry.) A review of your life is now being prepared. Were you a successful experiment?
2. An imaginary book called *Demon Summoning for Fun and Profit*.
3. The obscure obelisk that has mysteriously appeared in the center of campus.

Develop your essay using the steps outlined in Chapter Three: begin with brainstorming and then move on to an outline.

CHAPTER 5

THE MONSTER LIVES! ... OR DOES IT?

(Revision, Peer Reviewing, Retroactive Outlining)

SO, YOU'VE DONE YOUR EXPERIMENT! GO YOU! YOU'RE DONE NOW, RIGHT?

Sorry to be the bearer of bad news; however, what we know from scientists both mad and sane is that experiments often go awry and have to be tweaked and repeated multiple times before success is achieved (this is often how sane scientists end up mad!). It's the same with college compositions. The first draft is seldom the final draft.

It is important to note that this isn't just a student thing. The writing process on every level involves drafting, feedback, and revision. Even professional writers have editors, and the peer review process often entails revision. In fact, it often happens that more time is spent in revision than on the initial drafting of a document!

Part of the reason editing and revising is such a central part of the composition process is because when we write something, we already know what we're trying to say (at least, most of the time). Because of this, it isn't always clear to us when we haven't expressed something clearly. I think it is fair to say that we are inevitably the worst readers of our own work—I know from my own experience that I can read over the same page multiple times and just not see that that I've repeated or omitted a word, when someone else can pick out my mistake right away.

With this in mind, this chapter will address three important steps in the composition process that often don't get as much attention as drafting: self-review, peer reviewing, and revising.

Self-Review

Preliminary to peer reviewing and/or submission of your essay, you can save yourself some grief and embarrassment (and avoid looking like a doofus [again, sorry for the technical language]) by taking the following steps before having someone review your essay and/or submitting it for evaluation.

1. Look over the assignment instructions and requirements. Have you followed them?
2. If your assignment is an argumentative one, can you state your thesis clearly? See if you can finish this sentence: "In this essay, I argue that ..."
3. Thinking in terms of the thesis, is it one that needs to be argued? Or is it obvious to anyone with even a basic understanding of your topic? (If it "goes without saying"— that is, if it is obvious—then the thesis needs some adjusting.)
4. What support have you introduced to prove your argument? Do you have enough?
5. Look at the parts of your essay: is the argument that you present at the start what you actually end up arguing in the body of the essay? Does your conclusion reflect the argument introduced at the start? Consider drafting a *retroactive outline* to make sure organization is logical and effective. (See page 153).
6. Have you made clear to your reader why your position matters? If your reader gets to the end of your essay and says, "OK, so what?" do you have an answer? Remember: there should be a point to your essay!
7. Are you aware of how readers who disagree with your position might respond, and have you attempted to answer those criticisms?
8. Importantly, have you cited your sources consistently and completely throughout the body of the essay and, if appropriate, in a list of works cited at the end?

THE END APPROACHES ...

Now, add the necessary polish.

1. Make sure formatting conforms to assignment instructions.
2. Use spell check.
3. Don't assume spell check will catch all spelling errors. If you've misspelled "important" as "impotent" throughout your essay, spell check won't catch this because impotent is a correctly spelled word—just not the word you had in mind. And on some occasions, spell check will correct a misspelled word to something other than you intended.
4. **Read your essay out loud.**

Step 4 is the one often neglected, and it is the one most likely to help you catch little mistakes. I guarantee that reading out loud will help you hear errors that your eyes miss. You may initially feel silly—get over it. Or do it in the bathroom with the shower running. But read your paper out loud before turning it in. You'll thank me later.

5. If you are emailing or uploading an electronic file, give the file a specific file name that connects it to you.

You know what "essay 2" is on your computer. But once that file goes someplace else, it is easy for a file called "essay 2" to get lost—especially by someone who may have received multiple files with the same name. Avoid confusion and help make sure that you get the credit for your work by renaming your file something specific. Rather than "essay 2," I might try "Weinstock Essay 2 ENG 101 Fall 2018.docx."

And when you submit a revised file, update the file name to avoid confusion. For my assignment, I might go with "Weinstock Essay 2 ENG 101 Fall 2018 R1.docx"

The Perilous and Painful
Process of Peer Review

I hate to say it, but in my experience many students (excluding smart, good-looking ones like you, of course) don't really embrace the peer review process. They often make a good-faith effort at participating but feel they don't benefit substantially from the feedback they receive.

There are a number of reasons for the perception that the process is unnecessary or unhelpful, which range from a misunderstanding of the goals of the activity to rushed reviews to timid reviewers. Let's start with the justifications for the process itself:

- Yes, peer review is ideally intended to supply you with helpful feedback that you can use to improve your essay. However,
- Perhaps even more importantly, peer reviewing helps *you* become a better writer because it requires you to look critically at the work of other authors. *You become a better reader of your own work by looking at the work of your peers with a close eye.*

A primary goal of peer reviewing is to learn to think about your own writing in relation to the writing of others. If you read an essay that you feel is very effective, it can serve as a model or provide inspiration for your writing. And if you read something that you feel comes up short, that can highlight pitfalls to be aware of in your own writing as well. So, whether you get insightful feedback on your own paper or not, the process of *giving* feedback is still very valuable in itself.

Of course, ideally you want to supply—and to receive— useful feedback that can assist you in making your writing as effective as possible (and to get the best grade possible on the assignment, of course). Here then are some general tips on how to peer review the work of others:

1. *Do your best not to rush.* The more care you put into your evaluation, the more useful it will be to the author.
2. *Annotate as you go along.* If you have a hard copy, write on that sucker. If you have a digital copy, use the "insert comment" function to make comments. *Pay particular attention to moments where the meaning isn't clear to you.* The best feedback you can provide is to highlight moments where the writing is unclear. Remember—it's often hard for a writer to see where what they wrote fails to capture what they meant to say, and your most important job as a peer reviewer is to show them those spots so they can fix them. It's also nice to highlight what you think works well. The idea here is to give the writer a sense of how you experienced the essay as a reader.
3. *Don't mistake the trees for the forest.* That is, focus on the bigger picture first. Is the paper you read appropriate for the assignment? Does it answer the question being asked or respond to the assignment prompt? (If, for example, the assignment is to use a short reading as the impetus or "jumping off point" for the author's personal reflections, and the essay omits the reflective part, this is something your peer review should highlight!) Does the paper make sense? Does it skip around from idea to idea without firm connections? Does it miss something important? Does it misunderstand an assigned reading for the course? Don't be the reviewer who offers small comments and suggestions, but fails to point out that the essay itself is incomplete or doesn't meet assignment expectations in a significant way!

4. As a corollary to #3, *don't sweat the small stuff on a first draft.* If you notice a pattern of grammatical errors, you can certainly point that out, but (unless your instructor tells you something different) your job when peer reviewing is mainly to help the author improve organization and clarity, not necessarily to correct grammar and mechanics.

On now to the nuts and bolts of peer reviewing. As you undertake this process, bear in mind that *it is your job as a peer reviewer to be critical.* Your goal, of course, is never to be gratuitously mean; however, a peer review helps no one if it only says "good job!" and "this is great!" because the reviewer is too concerned about hurting the author's feelings. If you are overly timid, you've failed to help the person you've been assigned to help make their work stronger. The writer whose work you're reviewing won't know how to improve unless you point out aspects and parts of the essay that are weak.

If you aren't sure if something needs to be addressed, you can ask your instructor about it—or you can insert a comment that says something like "this doesn't seem appropriate for this assignment to me, but you may want to check with our fantastic professor before making changes." *It is better to call something that may be a problem to the author's attention and indicate that you are unsure, than it is just to say nothing.*

Bearing in mind the general tips above, here then are some additional questions that can guide you as you evaluate someone else's writing. (Depending on the type of assignment being evaluated, not all of these may apply.)

I. Start by reading the introductory paragraph or paragraphs and then answer these questions:

1. Do you know the general topic to be addressed by the essay? If it is about particular texts (books, films, etc.), has the author introduced the names of these texts and their creators?
2. Is there a clear and specific claim (thesis)? Write out for the author what you believe their thesis to be.
3. Is the thesis something that needs to be argued (that is, is it obvious)? Can the argument be supported (that is, is it ridiculous)?
4. Do you know after reading the first two paragraphs why the argument being made is worth making? That is, has the author told you why you should care?
5. Do you know after reading the first two paragraphs what the main points of the essay will be? Do you have a sense of how the essay will develop?

II. Now read the rest of the paper and answer these questions:

1. Is the essay submitted appropriate for the assignment? Does it conform to the instructions (including formatting)?
2. Does the paper make sense to you? Do you understand what the author is trying to do? Do the pieces seem to fit together? Are there parts that seem tangential or unclear?
3. What do you like most about the assignment? What seems to work best to you?
4. Compare the conclusion to the introduction: is the argument presented at the start actually the argument summed up in the conclusion? Do all the body paragraphs support this argument?
5. Having finished the essay, is it clear to you why the author's argument matters? Do you know why you should care?

6. Has the essay persuaded you? Why or why not? What would make the essay more persuasive?
7. Have any important ideas or points been omitted?
8. Has the author misunderstood something related to the assignment or class reading?
9. Does the essay make any claims that you feel are inaccurate, problematic, or under supported? If so, identify these.
10. Where support for the argument is introduced, has the author cited sources clearly and completely? (Since plagiarism, whether intentional or inadvertent, can have a dramatic impact on an assignment's grade, this is an important question!)
11. Are quotations incorporated into the author's own sentences with signal phrases?
12. Does the organization of the essay make sense to you? Do the points seem to appear in a logical order? Can you think of a way to improve organization?
13. Does the discussion feel balanced? That is, does the author allot the appropriate amount of attention to each major point?
14. Are paragraphs focused? Do any of them go on for more than a page? Are there lots of very short paragraphs strung together? Are transitions used between paragraphs?
15. Has the paper been spell checked? Do you note any recurring mechanical errors?

RE-VISION

Beware the Lazy First Draft!

If rather than making a good-faith effort at completing a solid first draft of an assignment, someone instead slaps together something half-baked at the eleventh hour just to have something to submit for peer review, that person has:

- Forfeited the chance to get useful feedback (because a peer reviewer can't really give specific or useful feedback on something half-baked).
- Left themselves a lot more work on the second draft (and we all get less busy as the semester moves forward, right?).
- And, frankly, disrespected the person doing the peer review, who now has to wade through the [censored] submitted and try to find something helpful to say—that is, the peer reviewer has to waste their time putting more thought into a response than went into the assignment—and none of us has time to waste.

Peer feedback is not intended to replace the author's own work on their writing! I know that you, good-looking and intelligent person that you are, would never do something like this, but, sadly, it happens.

How to cheat at Peek-a-boo.

Portrait of the instructor when they have to put more time into grading an essay than the author did into writing it.

Since this is about you, however, we'll assume that you made a good-faith effort at a solid first draft and have now received some thoughtful feedback on it. What are your next steps?

1. First things first: read over the feedback received and consider what seems most important to address.

You'll often receive more feedback than you can implement into a revision; on occasion (particularly if you have two readers of your assignment), you may get conflicting feedback, with one person highlighting something as a problem that the other doesn't note or in fact praises. So, it is up to you to decide what you feel needs to be revised and what doesn't.

2. Of course, you should automatically address the "no brainers," which include the following:

Fix the no-brainers.

- Your reviewer can't find or has misidentified your thesis.
- Your reviewer points out that the assignment you have submitted isn't in accordance with the assignment objectives or instructions. (This includes formatting.)
- Your reviewer points out places that are unclear.
- Your reviewer points out that you have misunderstood an important concept, omitted important points, or included points that undermine the argument you are making.
- Your reviewer points out that you haven't cited sources fully or correctly.
- Your reviewer points out missing words, incorrect words, mechanical errors, and so forth.

Few things are more irritating to an instructor than to see that a student received useful feedback on a first draft that was ignored. If these "no brainers" were pointed out on the first draft, but not addressed in the revision, what that tells me is that the student didn't bother to look at the feedback received—and that the reviewer wasted their time. I can't speak for other instructors, but that doesn't go over particularly well with me.

HONOR YOUR PEER REVIEWER'S INVESTMENT OF TIME AND EFFORT BY LOOKING OVER THE FEEDBACK SUPPLIED AND AT LEAST FIXING THE NO BRAINERS!

3. A competent revision seeks to improve *substance* as well as mechanics.

The revision activity described below—the *retroactive outline*—can be performed whether you have received feedback on a draft or not. However, a retroactive outline is a particularly useful approach to revision if you receive feedback indicating any of the following:

- overall organization is "loose," unclear, unbalanced, "bounces around," "needs tightening," and so on
- paragraphs are "loose" or unfocused

The Retroactive Outline

In Chapter Three, we discussed outlining. An outline is an extremely useful tool to help organize an essay prior to writing one. However, outlining can also be a useful technique to assist with reorganization after the fact. The process is as follows:

1. First, write out your essay's thesis.
2. Then outline the essay you have written. Make sure each new point in your essay has a corresponding point on the outline.
3. Consider the outline and look for ways to reorganize.

Return of the Dead: Revision in Action

What follows here is an example of a first draft of a student essay on monsters in Richard Matheson's 1954 novel *I Am Legend* and its 2007 film adaptation by Francis Lawrence. You'll see that evaluative feedback has been provided at the end. In response to the feedback, a retroactive outline has been prepared, and a second draft composed.

I Am Legend Film vs. Novel

The movie *I Am Legend* is very different from the novel, written by Richard Matheson, which it is based off of. Richard Matheson's *I Am Legend* was written in the 1950's, and the movie, directed by Francis Lawrence, was released in 2007. This creates a lot of differences just due to the time period in which they each were created. This difference allows each piece to portray the same concept in a way that makes the most sense during that period in time.

> Be more specific here. What are the differences to be discussed? And what is the concept you are referring to?

The movie *I Am Legend* does not portray the monsters as vampires, like Matheson does in his novel. In the movie, they are portrayed as mutant creatures that basically look like humans, except with no hair and their skin is a greyish color. The mutant creatures also cannot form words, the only way they speak is through somewhat of a growl/scream. In Matheson's novel, Robert Neville refers to the monsters as vampires, and some can actually speak words. For example, Ben Cortman, who was Robert Neville's neighbor, speaks to Neville every night. An example of this is on page 6, when it becomes night time, and the vampires start to surround Neville's house, Matheson writes, "Ben Cortman was shouting. 'Come out, Neville!'" In the novel, there are also two types of vampires: living

> It might make more sense to address the works chronologically.

This paragraph as a whole bounces back and forth between the film and the novel and addresses different points. Consider breaking it up into separate paragraphs.

This isn't correct. They do try to get in, which is why his house is barricaded, and he has to repair any damage each morning.

Your attention to detail is great!

No need to repeat this.

and dead. The character of Ruth, who is introduced in the fifteenth chapter of the novel, is a living vampire. She carries on normal conversations with Robert Neville and acts like a normal human-being. In the movie, there is only one type of monster, which is a mutant human, and there are also dogs with the same mutant disease. This change makes the monsters more monstrous in the movie because they look like mutated creatures that can't speak, which is harder to relate to. They also have far more strength in the movie, and they have no idea where Neville lives up until the end, when they destroy his house. In the novel, the vampires know exactly where Neville lives, but they don't try to destroy his house or attack him, unless he comes outside. The vampires just taunt him every night outside of his house. Another way that the monsters differ, is in the novel, the vampires hide and sleep during the day.

In the movie, they are shown in an abandoned warehouse, very much awake, feeding on something. They do not lay in houses, in a coma, like in the novel. These differences portrayed in the film, directed by Francis Lawrence, contribute to the overall modern and futuristic feel. The film appeals to the modern audience, who is expecting a futuristic horror film with monsters. The alternate ending to the movie, *I Am Legend*, which I watched, shows that the monsters are actually intelligent creatures who can feel, and have a system with a leader. This also contributes to the modernism by making them so advanced when, in the novel, they are thought to be stupid, mindless vampires.

> This point seems important, but questionable to me— we don't find out the vampires are really intelligent in either the book or the film until the end.

Another aspect of the film, that makes it a modernized version of the novel, is the technology and weapons that are used. In the novel, Neville uses wooden stakes to kill the vampires. On page 17, Matheson writes, "After lunch, he went from house to house and used up all his stakes. He had forty-seven stakes." This is talking about how Neville went out during the day, from house to house, to kill vampires, while they were sleeping, with his individual wooden stakes that he hand-made. Neville came to the conclusion, in the novel, that the vampires cannot be killed with guns, because the bullets just get absorbed into the skin and have no effect. On pages 129–130, Neville explains why the bullets don't work on the vampires; Matheson writes, "Through experiments on the dead vampires he had discovered that the bacilli effected the creation of a powerful body glue that sealed bullet openings as soon as they were made. Bullets were enclosed almost immediately, and since the system was activated by germs, a bullet couldn't hurt it." However, in the movie, Robert Neville only uses guns to kill the monsters. This is a big example in the modernism of the movie, because hand-made wooden stakes

> This also feels important.

> A little confusing here—what do you mean by "modernism"? (this could get confused with modernism as a genre)

would have been very old-fashioned. In many action and horror films today, guns are the main weapon used to kill off the "bad guys" or "monsters." The technology and resources that were used in the movie are also different from the novel. In the novel, Neville goes to the library to find books on blood and bacteria. On page 68, Matheson writes, "He pulled out five books on general physiology and several works on blood. These he stacked on one of the dust-surfaced tables. Should he get any of the books on bacteriology? He stood a minute, looking indecisively at the buckram backs. Finally he shrugged. Well, what's the difference? He thought. They can't do any harm. He pulled out several of them at random and added them to the pile. He now had nine books on the table." This was the source of all the knowledge that he gained, to try to find a cure for the virus. The only instrument that he uses is a microscope, which he barely knows how to use. In the film, Neville has a lab in his basement with many, many tools and instruments. He has a video camera that he uses to record his findings daily, and he also has access to rats that he uses to experiment on. As an audience member, one doesn't know how he gained all of this information, but the movie starts off with him already having tried many different potential cures, and already knowing how to use all of the tools in his lab. He

I think we are told that he is an army virologist, which would explain how he gained this information. You might want to check this point.

is portrayed as a very intelligent man who is determined to find the cure.

In conclusion, the 2007 film, *I Am Legend*, is a modernized version of the novel, *I Am Legend*, written by Richard Matheson. Both the novel and the film portray a futuristic version of the world, relative to the time period in which each work was released/published, in which mankind is nearly destroyed. The film appeals to the modern day audience by using modern day advanced weapons and technology, and making the monsters look, sound, and act more monstrous.

Feedback: This is an interesting essay that does a great job with detail! You clearly show the ways the novel and film are parallel and where they part ways. What I think would make it even stronger is some attention to argument and organization.

Right now, I'm not totally clear what your argument is, other than that there are similarities and differences having to do with the period in which each version was made. You then point these out, but it isn't always clear to me in what way the differences are meaningful and how the differences are connected to the time period. Maybe you could make the argument specifically about the role of technology? And would it be worth exploring that the vampires in the novel seem to result from nuclear war while the vampires in the film are the result of a virus?

The other thing I notice is that there is a lot of bouncing around within paragraphs. Paragraphs 2 and 3 each are long and shift around a lot. So I would recommend you try to clarify your argument and then look to organization. Nice work so far!

I Am Legend: Film vs. Novel
Retroactive Outline

I. Introduction
   A. Introduce texts
   B. Differences due to time period
   C. Same concept

II. Paragraph 2: General Comparison
   A. Film: monsters not vampires but mutants
   B. Film: cannot speak
   C. Novel: monsters called vampires
   D. Novel: some can speak
   E. Novel: two types of vampires: living and dead
   F. Film: one kind of vampire
   G. Film: also, dogs as vampires
   H. Lack of speech makes film vampires more monstrous
   I. Film: vampires are stronger
   J. Film: vampires don't know where Neville lives until the end
   K. Novel: vampires know where he lives all along
   L. Novel: vampires sleep during the day
   M. Film: awake during the day
   N. Differences make the film more modern
      1. Film: vampires intelligent
      2. Novel: vampires seem stupid until the end.

III. Paragraph 3: Technology
   A. Novel: wooden stakes
   B. Film: guns
   C. Novel: Neville a non-expert
      1. Library
      2. Microscope
   D. Film: Neville as expert

I Am Legend: Film vs. Novel (Revised)

The movie *I Am Legend* is very different from the novel, written by Richard Matheson, which it is based off of. Richard Matheson's *I Am Legend* was written in the 1950's, and the movie, directed by Francis Lawrence, was released in 2007. While Lawrence retains Matheson's surprising conclusion that the vampires aren't the mindless creatures Robert Neville assumes them to be, he updates the monsters, the technology, and the cause of the disease to reflect the expectations and anxieties of modern audiences.

In Matheson's novel, Robert Neville refers to the monsters as vampires, and they sleep during the day. They seem generally humanlike and all of them can speak. For example, Ben Cortman, who was Robert Neville's neighbor, speaks to Neville every night. An example of this is on page 6, when it becomes night time, and the vampires start to surround Neville's house, Matheson writes, "Ben Cortman was shouting. 'Come out, Neville!'" In the novel, however, it is revealed that there are also two types of vampires: living and dead. The character of Ruth, who is introduced in the fifteenth chapter of the novel, is a living vampire. She carries on normal conversations with Robert Neville and acts like a normal human being. The living vampires, which Neville has been killing along with the dead ones, have been developing their own society and think of Neville as the monster who comes while they sleep.

Lawrence's film version of the novel enhances the monstrosity of the vampires, which not only makes the film scarier, but makes the surprise at the end that the vampires aren't simply monsters without feelings that much more effective. In the movie, the monsters are portrayed as mutant creatures that basically look like humans, except with no hair and their skin is a grayish color. They are extremely strong, and do not sleep during the day. Instead, they are shown in an abandoned warehouse, very much awake, feeding on something. They do not lay in houses, in a coma, like in the novel. Importantly, the mutant creatures also cannot form words; the only way they speak is through somewhat of a growl/scream. This change makes the monsters more monstrous in the movie because they look like mutated creatures that can't speak, which is harder to relate to.

All these changes in the film make the vampires seem much more animalistic and monstrous than in the novel. As Neville struggles to survive and to find a cure, we excuse his experimentation on the vampires because they are monsters out to destroy him and for whom we feel little sympathy. This sets the audience up to be surprised and to rethink their assumptions once it is revealed in the alternative ending that the vampires do have feelings and that the leader is seeking the female on whom Neville has been experimenting.

Another aspect of the novel updated by the film is the technology and weapons that are used. In the novel, it is implied that the vampire plague is a result of nuclear war. Neville is not an expert on vampires or viruses, but in fact uses the library and a microscope to do research. Neville, for example, works out why stakes are effective at killing vampires but bullets are not: "Through experiments on the dead vampires he had discovered that the bacilli effected the creation of a powerful body glue that sealed bullet openings as soon as they were made. Bullets were enclosed almost immediately, and since the system was activated by germs, a bullet couldn't hurt it" (129– 30). Stakes, in contrast, keep the wound open.

In Lawrence's film, Neville is recast as a U.S. Army virologist and, reflecting contemporary anxieties, the vampire plague is the result of a vaccine for cancer that goes wrong. Neville has a lab in his basement with many, many tools and instruments. He has a video camera that he uses to record his findings daily, and he also has access to rats that he uses to experiment on. Like Neville in the novel, he is intent on finding a cure for the vampire plague. The cause of the plague, however, has been altered to reflect modern anxieties, and Neville's tools have been updated to make the film seem modern.

In conclusion, the 2007 film, *I Am Legend*, is a modernized version of the novel, *I Am Legend*, written by Richard Matheson. Both the novel and the film portray a futuristic version of the world relative to the time period in which each work was released/published in which mankind is nearly destroyed. The film appeals to the modern day audience by making the monsters look, sound, and act more monstrous, and by introducing contemporary weapons and technology. The film also updates the cause of the vampire plague to reflect modern anxieties. However, despite these differences, the film retains Matheson's trick ending that forces the audience to reconsider just who the monster is.

YOUR TURN: RETROACTIVE REVISING

Using the peer reviewing approach and questions outlined above, first evaluate the student essay below on *Frankenstein*. Then prepare a retroactive outline that could be used as a step toward revision.

The Monstrosity Society Animates

Mary Shelley's *Frankenstein* is a novel which has been used as the base for horror films about a monster who is created by a mad scientist. This monster is named Frankenstein in the modern-day adaptations of the classic novel and wreaks havoc through cities killing everything in sight. Until the heroic scientist kills Frankenstein-the-monster and saves the city. However, this plot is different than the original novel. In the novel, Victor Frankenstein is the scientist who creates the monster. In fact, the monster is never named in the story; instead it is referred to as "daemon," "the creature," or "the monster." The monster in the novel is not immediately drawn to evil acts like the movie versions portray. The monster in the novel only becomes dangerous after being rejected and isolated from the rest of humanity. This questions whether the monster in the novel is innately evil or if society has shunned the monster toward evil behaviors.

The monster's hardships began as soon as the monster is brought into the world by Frankenstein. When the monster is first reanimated, Frankenstein runs away in fright from the creation, "Unable to endure the aspect of the being I had created, I rushed out of the room ..." (58). This is the first memory the monster has of its creator. As a scientist, Frankenstein believed he failed and created a horrible monster and immediately regretted his work. The monster grew to hate Frankenstein because Frankenstein abandoned the monster before the monster had time to prove its genuine lust for human knowledge and companionship. Later in the novel, the monster demanded Frankenstein build the monster a female companion. By having another creation who resembled the monster, the monster would no longer be alone in the world without a being to call his friend. Frankenstein decided to rip apart the female before her reanimation, damning the monster once again into isolation.

During the first couple of months after the monster's creation, the monster does not do any sort of malicious deed. Instead, the monster's life is characterized by trying to understand human nature and how to be more like the humans who surround him. The monster becomes well educated after he observed a family who lived in a cottage, "the cottagers" as the monster called them, near the woods where the monster called home (114). During this time in isolation, the monster learned how to speak and read just as any other human would. In doing so, the monster proves that it can assimilate into society and conform to the social norms and can be a functioning member of society. Which shows the monster did not initially want to do harm to any human, it wanted to be a part of the human world. The monster became comfortable enough to emerge from the woods and confronted the family he admired dearly, but instead was met with disgust and hate. The monster was beaten by one of the cottagers and soon fled from the cottage and banished himself to isolation once more.

The monster portrays not only human characteristics, but also portrays human beliefs and human compassion. Page 143 of the text shows the gentle and human side of the monster when he saves a little girl who is drowning. This heroic act is done after the monster is rejected by the cottagers, meaning the monster hoped that society could accept him. That maybe, by doing a good deed, society would be able to see through the monster's ugly exterior and see the compassion the monster has learned to have. By saving the little girl, the reader is inclined to question whether the monster is truly a monster. Monsters typically do not save people; they harm them. This human-like tendency allows readers to sympathize more with the monster because it is shown the monster truly wants to be like every other human. However, society does not allow the monster to live in the luxuries of humanity. Instead, the reward the monster receives for saving the little girl is getting shot by the little girl's father, which is the monster's final rejection from society before beginning his vengeance quest against Frankenstein.

It is because the abandonment and isolation the monster began to wreak havoc in Frankenstein's life, not because the monster was born with evil tendencies. Exclusion from Frankenstein and the cottagers give the monster a feeling that no person ever wants to feel; loneliness. Frankenstein

and society forced the monster into isolation, which made the monster lead a lonely life. The monster just wanted a companion so it would never be lonely again, but Frankenstein denies the monster of this companionship. After watching the growing relationships of humans from the constraints of the forest, the monster desires a companion that will allow him happiness like every other human. The monster believes that he deserves a companion because the monster has grown to be just like other humans. Due to society being unaccepting of the monster due to his frightening appearance, the monster only yearns to be relinquished from his loneliness by having a companion.

YOUR TURN: THE RETROACTIVE OUTLINE

Two sample student essays are included as appendices at the end of this guide. Create a retroactive outline of one or both of them. Identify the thesis, outline the main points, and then consider if you think there are ways to improve organization.

The Error Log

The ultimate goal of any composition course is improvement as skills are introduced and reinforced. One tool that can assist you in adding polish to your writing is an **error log**. An error log is a kind of diary of mistakes that have been called to your attention, as well as methods of addressing them.

Here's how to create an error log:

1. Use a notebook or create a document. Title it something dramatic like "Death Lurks Within These Pages" or "I Will Never Love Again."

2. Look at the feedback you've received from your instructor and make entries in your error log that identify errors. Pay particular attention to errors that are indicated as repeated.
3. Look for patterns—what mistakes do you tend to make most often?
4. Indicate how you would correct the error.

SENTENCE	ERROR TYPE	CORRECTED
At the start, Victor was a fresh-faced young lad; ready to tackle the world.	Misuse of semicolon. Don't use it where a period couldn't replace it.	At the start, Victor was a fresh-faced young lad, ready to tackle the world.
In "Frankenstein," Victor was a scientist who attempted to create a living being out of pieces of corpses.	Use present tense to summarize what happens in a novel (MLA rule).	In *Frankenstein*, Victor is a scientist who attempts to create a living being out of pieces of corpses.
In "Frankenstein," Victor was a scientist who attempted to create a living being out of pieces of corpses.	Italicize titles of novels.	In *Frankenstein*, Victor is a scientist who attempts to create a living being out of pieces of corpses.

One last thought here about editing, the revision process, and improvement: speaking from experience, few things are more discouraging to an instructor (and more likely to result in an unhappy outcome for a student), than when students continue to make the same errors called to their attention all semester long. If you are making the same mistakes at the end of the course that you made at the beginning, then something has gone wrong—either the instructor has not clearly identified the error and shown you how to fix it, or you haven't paid attention to the feedback or tried to implement it, or some combination of the two things.

The error log can help you avoid this unfortunate outcome. Yes, it takes effort. But understanding how to identify and correct different kinds of mistakes can help you avoid them. It will add polish to your writing, making it more effective at achieving your overall goals.

YOUR TURN: FURTHER EVALUATION

Consider one or both of the sample student essays included as appendices at the back of this guide, and evaluate their strengths and weaknesses. What do you find most and least persuasive and why? What aspects of the essay(s) could you see incorporating into your own writing?

CHAPTER 6

PLACATING GHOSTS

*(Systems of Citing Sources to Avoid Angering
the Dead ... and the Living)*

AS WAS EMPHASIZED IN CHAPTER TWO, PLAGIARISM IS THE presentation of the words or ideas of someone else as though they are your own. It's a form of theft and angers both the dead and the living. (And if horror films teach us anything, it's don't anger the dead! What life teaches us, however, is that angering the living often doesn't work out terribly well either.)

Obviously, a smart and good-looking person such as yourself would never intentionally plagiarize. And this chapter, together with Chapter Two, is intended to help you avoid inadvertent plagiarism by outlining how to cite sources fully and correctly.

Maddeningly, a number of different systems have been developed to cite sources. The point of having different systems is, of course, *to create confusion for you and others* (and let's not even get started on publishing houses that have their own in-house systems for citations that combine elements of the major systems).

All citation systems however consist of two parts: identification of material taken from a source within the body of the text, and then a complete citation in a note or list of works cited.

The goals are to clearly identify words and language that aren't the author's own, and to provide all the information another researcher might need to find the same quoted or referenced material.

Let me add that, while the different citation systems have very specific formatting requirements—and you should try your best to pay attention to the details and get it right—minor errors can be fixed. *The vital thing is to avoid plagiarism by making it clear when words and ideas aren't your own, and then attributing them to their sources.* With that in mind, it's better to be overly zealous in citing your sources than to be lax about it and get yourself in hot water!

Italics vs. Quotation Marks:
A Battle to the Death for the Ages

Before getting into the details of the primary systems of citation used, a quick word about indicating titles (and this applies across the board, not just for bibliographies or lists of works cited). So how do you know whether to use italics or quotation marks?

To make a determination, ask this question: Is the source a part of something bigger?

- If a source is *not* a small part of something larger, then render the title using *italics*. (Use underlining in place of italics only if writing by hand or, having made use of a time machine, you are working on an old-fashioned manual typewriter that can't do italics!)
- If a source *is* a small part of something larger, render the title using "quotation marks."

ITALICS	"QUOTATION MARKS"
Book title	Chapter title
Journal, Magazine, Newspaper, or Periodical Title	Essays, articles, or entries within a larger work
Film	
Television show	Episode of a television show
Album	Song
Web site (homepage)	Subsidiary page of web site

- In general, titles are indicated by using either italics *or* quotation marks, not both. The exception is the title of a book that includes the title of a short story such as *Approaches to Teaching Charlotte Perkins Gilman's "The Yellow Wallpaper."*
- As noted in Chapter Two, in North American English, double quotation marks are used in all cases except to indicate a quotation within a quotation. This exception sometimes comes up in journal articles addressing a particular short story such as James Gargano's essay, "Poe's 'Ligeia': Dream and Destruction."
- Also, as noted in Chapter One, in North American English, periods and commas are placed inside quotation marks not following them. Note the placement of the period in this citation: "Pregnant Women and Envious Men in 'Morella,' 'Berenice,' 'Ligeia,' and 'The Fall of the House of Usher.'" In North American English, commas and periods always go inside all quotation marks.
- The British system is the reverse of the North American system where quotation marks and punctuation placement are concerned. (Where punctuation is concerned, the British system makes more sense.)

Getting Stylish: MLA, APA, Chicago, and OUIJA

I will now offer an overview of the main citation systems you are likely to be called on to use. (If you thought Chapter One on mechanics was fun, you ain't seen nothing yet!)

What I'll be outlining here are general rules for the different systems of citation and then providing templates for common types of sources. *This guide does not cover every single type of source you might encounter.* Luckily, the organizations that create these rules have comprehensive guides; I also recommend the Purdue University Online Writing Lab (OWL) as a resource for formatting instructions for less common sources.

Use caution when using programs and websites that generate bibliographies and works cited!

These can be useful tools, but they require you to correctly identify the type of source and to supply the proper information!

MONSTERS LOVE ASPARAGUS (AKA MLA)

MLA

MLA, which also stands for the Modern Language Association, is the format most commonly used for citing sources within the humanities and liberal arts. Additional guidelines can be found in the *MLA Handbook*. The guidelines below conform to the 8th edition of this handbook. (The 8th edition made some significant changes—if you consult an earlier edition of the *MLA Handbook* or an older style guide, you'll see some differences. My personal feeling is that as long as you are consistent, it doesn't really matter which edition you are using; as always though, check with your instructor—because they are the person evaluating your work, not me!)

I. How to Cite Material within the Body of the Text Using MLA

MLA employs what is called **parenthetical citation**. What this means is that you include information in parentheses in the body of the text that identifies your source and directs your reader to a list of works cited at the end for the full citation. *What's important here is that the way you identify your source in the body of the text must correlate exactly with an entry in your works cited at the end.*

Let's say you include a quotation from Mathias Clasen's book, *Why Horror Seduces*, in your research paper. You would cite the source parenthetically in the body of the text like this:

- "The horror genre ... achieves its peculiar affective goal by targeting an evolved defense system, the fear system" (Clasen 29).

This parenthetical citation tells the reader that the quotation comes from Clasen and appears on page 29. Note that there is *not* a comma between Clasen and 29, just a space, and that end punctuation for the quotation has been shifted to the right so that it follows the parentheses. Note as well that you do *not* include "page" or "p." You just include the name and the page number, separated by a space.

The reader then looks to the list of works cited at the end to find a corresponding entry for Clasen that provides the complete citation:

Clasen, Mathias. *Why Horror Seduces*. Oxford University Press, 2017.

Artist's interpretation of the author when students haven't cited sources.

Things are even easier if you have already introduced the author in the body of the text. In this case, you simply provide the page number:

- In Mathias Clasen's study of horror, he proposes that "the horror genre ... achieves its peculiar affective goal by targeting an evolved defense system, the fear system" (29).

Only provide the author's name in the parentheses to clarify. If you've already mentioned in the sentence who the author is, you don't need to repeat this in the parentheses.

E-BOOKS

Citing an e-book or Kindle version can be a little tricky. The main goal is always to provide enough information to help someone else find the same passage you are quoting or moment you are referencing.

If the book includes some kind of built-in numbering system that tells users where they are in the book, use that—this could include explicit paragraph numbers, location numbers, or chapter numbers. The important thing is that whatever you use has to be standard across different devices. Never count paragraphs or pages or make up a numbering system yourself. If there are no page, chapter, paragraph, or section numbers in the original text, then no numbers should be included with the citation. You would just do it like this:

- "The horror genre ... achieves its peculiar affective goal by targeting an evolved defense system, the fear system" (Clasen).

The works cited would then make clear that this is a Kindle edition:

Clasen, Mathias. *Why Horror Seduces*. Kindle ed., Oxford University Press, 2017.

UNKNOWN AUTHOR

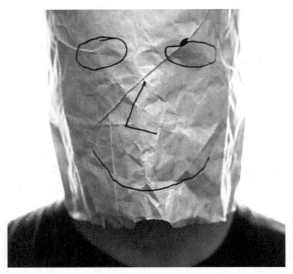

If the author isn't known, then you supply in the parentheses *a shortened version of the title* of the work from which you have taken language or information. This, again, will correspond unambiguously to a complete citation in the works cited at the end.

Let's say you quote from the Wikipedia page on basilisks. The parenthetical citation would look like this:

- According to the Wikipedia page, the basilisk "is a legendary reptile reputed to be a serpent king who can cause death with a single glance" ("Basilisk").

Since the Wikipedia page has no author, you identify the source in the body of the text by the name of the article.[1] There then must be a complete citation corresponding to this in the works cited:

"Basilisk." *Wikipedia, The Free Encyclopedia*, 20 May 2018, https://en.wikipedia.org/wiki/Basilisk. Accessed 30 May 2018.

MORE THAN ONE WORK BY THE SAME AUTHOR

If you are working with more than one work by the same author, it is important to distinguish which work is being cited. You do this by including part of the title in the parentheses. Let's say you are writing an essay on the Harry Potter books, and quote from more than one of them. You would indicate your source like this:

- According to Rowling's Professor Lupin, "The patronus is a kind of positive force, a projection of the very things that the dementor feeds upon – hope, happiness, the desire to survive – but it cannot feel despair, as real humans can, so the dementors can't hurt it" (*Prisoner of Azkaban* 237).

There would then be a corresponding entry for *Harry Potter and the Prisoner of Azkaban* in the works cited.

---

1 Wikipedia tells you to identify all sources as being authored by "Wikipedia contributors." Ignore this and go with what I'm telling you here. The reason I'm telling you to ignore this is because listing the author as "Wikipedia Contributors" creates a ton of confusion if you refer to more than one Wikipedia source, and it also contradicts what MLA tells us to do for sources with unknown authors.

If it isn't made clear in the body of your text who the author of the referenced material is, then that must be indicated parenthetically as well. Let's say you are writing about monster plants and refer to several different Harry Potter books in the course of your discussion.

- Some horror narratives feature animate plants such as in this example: "The Whomping Willow was creaking and lashing out with its lower branches" (Rowling, *Prisoner of Azkaban* 404).

Note that here a comma separates the author's last name from an abbreviated version of the title.

> The key thing here in all cases is to make sure you've identified the source in the body of the text (with a page number, where one exists) and indicated it in such a way that it corresponds directly to an entry in the works cited.

II. Works Cited Templates for MLA (8th edition)

Here is how to cite different types of commonly used sources using MLA (the 8th edition).

> **Note**: for books sources of all types, MLA requires the city of publication to be included only if the work was published prior to 1900.

A BOOK

Last Name, First Name. *Title of Book*. Publisher, Publication Date.

Heller, Terry. *The Delights of Terror: An Aesthetics of the Tale of Terror*. University of Illinois Press, 1987.

If the source was published prior to 1900, MLA asks that the city in which the source was published be included:

Last Name, First Name. *Title of Book*. City of Publication: Publisher, Publication Date.

Dickens, Charles. *A Tale of Two Cities*. London: Chapman & Hall, 1859.

A CHAPTER IN AN EDITED COLLECTION OR ANTHOLOGY

For whatever reason, this one often throws students for a loop. As mentioned in Chapter Two, an editor is someone who assembles contributions by different authors. An edited collection or anthology then is a book that collects together in one place contributions by many different authors. The important part here is that, both in the body of the text and in the list of works cited at the end, you cite *the author* of the chapter.

Last Name, First Name. "Title of Chapter." *Title of Collection*, edited by Name(s) of Editor(s), Publisher, Year, page range of entry.

Weinstock, Jeffrey Andrew. "Postmodernism with Sam Raimi (or, How I Learned to Stop Worrying About Theory and Love *Evil Dead*)." *Fear and Learning: Essays on the Pedagogy of Horror*, edited by Aalya Ahmad and Sean Moreland, McFarland & Company, 2013, pp. 19–39.

AN ARTICLE OR ESSAY IN A SCHOLARLY JOURNAL

Journals typically have *volume and issue numbers*—this information must be included. Titles of works that appear *within* the journal are identified using quotation marks. The journal itself (which is the "container") is identified by using italics.

Last Name, First Name. "Title of Article." *Title of Journal*, vol. number, issue no., Year, page range.

Arata, Stephen. "The Occidental Tourist: *Dracula* and the Anxiety of Reverse Colonization." *Victorian Studies*, vol. 33, no. 4, 1990, pp. 621–45.

AN ARTICLE IN A NEWSPAPER OR MAGAZINE

Last Name, First Name. "Title of Article." *Title of Periodical*, Day Month Year, page range.

Grossman, Lev. "Zombies Are the New Vampires." *Time Magazine*, 20 April 2009, p. 161.

A DOCTORAL DISSERTATION OR MASTER'S THESIS

As noted in Chapter Two, be careful with these kinds of sources, as they are not typically written for a general readership, or vetted or published in the traditional sense. Cite the source as you would a book, but include the designation "PhD dissertation" or "MA (or MS) thesis," followed by the degree-granting institution and the year awarded. It is important that you identify the source as a dissertation or thesis.

Last Name, First Name. *Title of Dissertation*. Year. University, Type of work.

Lauro, Sarah J. *The Modern Zombie: Living Death in the Technological Age*. 2011. University of California, Davis, PhD dissertation.

A REVIEW

As noted in Chapter Two, if you find a review of a book that seems useful to the research you are doing, get the book being reviewed rather than relying on the review!

Last Name, First Name. "Title of Review [if there is one]." Review of *Title of Work*, by Author/Director/Artist. *Title of Periodical*, Day Month Year, page range.

Macon, Caro. "'Monster Portraits': An Exploration of Identity That's Entirely Unique." Review of *Monster Portraits*, by Del Samatar and Sofia Samatar. *Los Angeles Review of Books*, 18 May 2018, https://lareviewofbooks.org/article/monster-portraits-an-exploration-of-identity-thats-entirely-unique#! Accessed 30 May 2018.

A PAGE ON A WEBSITE

Last Name, First Name [if known]. "Title of Page." *Title of Site*, date of page creation or last update, URL. Accessed Day Month Year.

Carrillo, Stephanie. "Why We Love Monsters." *Facing History and Ourselves*, 28 October 2014, http://lanetwork.facinghistory.org/why-we-love-monsters/. Accessed 30 May 2018.

AN ARTICLE FROM AN ONLINE DATABASE

Append database information after other information. DOIs (Digital Object Identifiers) are preferable to URLs (web addresses) because DOIs are more stable—and dead links are the bane of researchers everywhere!

Last Name, First Name. "Title of Article or Essay." *Title of Journal or Periodical*, vol., no., year, page range. *Database*, DOI or URL. Accessed Day Month Year.

O'Leary, Peter. "Sacred Fantasy in *Game of Thrones*." *Critical Quarterly*, vol. 57, no. 1, 2015, pp. 6–19. *ProQuest*, DOI: http://dx.doi.org/10.1111/criq.12174. Accessed 10 September 2019.

EMAIL

Last Name, First Name. "Subject Line." Received by First Name Last Name, Day Month Year.

Frankenstein, Victor. "Mad Scientist's Guide." Received by Jeffrey Weinstock, 31 October 2018.

A TWEET

Twitter handle. "Tweet in its entirety," *Twitter*, date of posting, time of posting, URL.

@VictorFrankenstein. "The Monster Lives," *Twitter*, 31 October 2018, 12:01 a.m., twitter.com/victorfrankenstein/ status/333666999234566?lang=en.

A YOUTUBE VIDEO

Author/Creator Last Name, First Name [if available]. "Title." *YouTube*, uploaded by First Name Last Name, Day Month Year uploaded, URL.

If the author/creator is the same as the person who uploaded the video, then list the name only once.

"Nightmare! The Birth of Victorian Horror: Dracula (Full programme, feat. Eileen Daly)." *YouTube*, uploaded by Eileen Daly (Official), 3 September 2012, https://www. youtube.com/watch?v=88edGlW3DT4&t=208s.

A FILM

Title. Directed by First Name Last Name, performances by First Name Last Name, film studio or distributor, year.

Get Out. Directed by Jordan Peele, performances by Daniel Kaluuya, Allison Williams, Universal Pictures, 2017.

A TV PROGRAM

"Episode Title." *Program Title*, written by First Name Last Name, directed by First Name Last Name, distributor name, date of distribution or first airing.

"Night Work." *Penny Dreadful*, written by John Logan, directed by J.A. Bayona, Showtime/Sky, 11 May 2014.

III. Sample List of Works Cited MLA *(8th edition)*

- Lists of works cited and bibliographies are always organized alphabetically by the lead author's last name or the title of works with unknown authors. *They are never numbered.*
- The first line of each entry should be flush with the left margin. Second and subsequent lines should be indented half an inch. *Works cited lists and bibliographies should never be centered.*
- When a source has more than one author, only the first author is listed last name first. The rest are listed first name first.
- If you have more than one source included by the same author, organize them alphabetically (ignore articles like "A," "An," and "The"). List the first one as you normally would with the author's name last name first. For the second and subsequent entries by the same author, replace the author's name with three hyphens and a period.

Asma, Stephen T. *On Monsters: An Unnatural History of Our Worst Fears*. Oxford University Press, 2009.

Cohen, Jeffrey Jerome. "Monster Theory (Seven Theses)." *Monster Theory: Reading Culture*, edited by Jeffrey Jerome Cohen, University of Minnesota Press, 1996, pp. 3–25.

Get Out. Directed by Jordan Peele, performances by Daniel Kaluuya, Allison Williams, Universal Pictures, 2017.

Mathijs, Ernest and Jamie Sexton. *Cult Cinema: An Introduction*. Wiley-Blackwell, 2011.

"Nightmare! The Birth of Victorian Horror: Dracula (Full programme, feat. Eileen Daly)." *YouTube*, uploaded by Eileen Daly (Official), 3 Sept. 2012, https://www.youtube.com/watch?v=88edGlW3DT4&t=208s.

"Night Work." *Penny Dreadful*, written by John Logan, directed by J.A. Bayona, Showtime/Sky, 11 May 2014.

Riefe, Jordan. "Guillermo del Toro: 'I love monsters the way people worship holy images.'" *The Guardian*, 3 August 2016, https://www.theguardian.com/film/2016/aug/03/guillermo-del-toro-bleak-house-home-lacma-exhibit. Accessed 31 May 2018.

Suzuki, Erin. "Beasts from the Deep." *Journal of Asian American Studies*, vol. 20, no. 1, 2017, pp. 11–28. *Project Muse*, https://doi.org/10.1353/jaas.2017.0002. Accessed 17 June 2017.

Weinstock, Jeffrey Andrew. *The Rocky Horror Picture Show*. Wallflower Press, 2008.

---. *The Vampire Film: Undead Cinema*. Columbia University Press, 2012.

AUDACIOUS PARANORMAL ASSOCIATION (AKA APA)

APA

OK, so APA actually means American Psychological Association and this citation style is most commonly used in the social sciences. This style is closer to MLA than Chicago, and makes use of an in-text author-date format. A complete citation is then provided at the end in a list of references.

I. How to Cite Material within the Body of the Text Using APA

Where information or language from other sources is introduced, the APA system requires you to make clear in the body of the text the author, the year of publication, and, for direct quotations, the page number.

The easiest way to do this is to introduce the author's name with a signal phrase, followed by the date of publication in parentheses:

- According to Halberstam (1995), monsters are "meaning machines" (p. 21).

If the author is not named in a signal phrase, then this information gets added to the parentheses:

- Monsters "can represent gender, race, nationality, class and sexuality in one body" (Halberstam, 1995, pp. 21–22).

In the APA system, page numbers are supplied only for direct quotations. To acknowledge paraphrases or ideas taken from other sources, only the author's name and date are required. When a page number is supplied, it is preceded by the letter p followed by a period (p.) or pp. if a quotation spans more than one page.

If the author is unknown, cite the source by its title in a signal phrase or use the first few words in the parentheses:

- According to the website "Zombies and the Women who Love them" (2012), ...

II. Works Cited Templates for APA (6th edition)

Here is how to cite different types of commonly used sources using APA. For more information, consult the *Publication Manual of the American Psychological Association*.

> **Note**: APA recommends "sentence style" capitalization in which most words of titles are lowercased. The rule is to capitalize the first word of the title, the first word of a subtitle, and, of course, proper nouns. Use lowercase for everything else.

A BOOK

Last Name, First and Middle Initials. (Year of Publication). *Title of work*. Location: Publisher.

Heller, T. (1987). *The delights of terror: An aesthetics of the tale of terror*. Carbondale, IL: University of Illinois Press.

A CHAPTER IN AN EDITED COLLECTION OR ANTHOLOGY

For whatever reason, this one often throws students for a loop. As mentioned in Chapter Two, an editor is someone who assembles contributions by different authors. An edited collection or anthology then is a book that collects together in one place contributions by many different authors. The important part here is that, both in the body of the text and in the list of works cited at the end, you cite *the author* of the chapter.

Last Name, First and Middle Initials. (Year of Publication). Title of chapter. In Name(s) of Editor(s) (Ed[s].), *Title of book* (pages of chapter). Location: Publisher.

Weinstock, J.A. (2013). Postmodernism with Sam Raimi (or, how I learned to stop worrying about theory and love *Evil dead*). In A. Ahmad & S. Moreland (Eds.), *Fear and learning: Essays on the pedagogy of horror* (pp. 19–39). Jefferson, NC: McFarland & Company.

AN ARTICLE OR ESSAY IN A SCHOLARLY JOURNAL

Last Name, First and Middle Initials. (Year). Title of article. *Title of Periodical, volume number*(issue number), page range. DOI or URL [if available].

Arata, S. (1990). The occidental tourist: *Dracula* and the anxiety of reverse colonization. *Victorian Studies, 33*(4), 621–45.

AN ARTICLE IN A MAGAZINE

Last Name, First and Middle Initials. (Year, Month Day). Title of
article. *Periodical Title, volume*(issue number), page range.

Grossman, L. (2009, April 09). Zombies are the new vampires.
Time Magazine, 173(15), 161.

AN ARTICLE IN A NEWSPAPER

Curiously, p. or pp. precedes page numbers for newspaper references in APA.

Last Name, First and Middle Initials. (Year, Month Day). Title of
article. *Title of Newspaper*, pp.

Dargis, M & Scott, A.O. (2017, May 5). At the movies: Our
monsters, ourselves. *The New York Times*, p. AR31.

A DOCTORAL DISSERTATION
OR MASTER'S THESIS

Last Name, First and Middle Initials. (Year). *Title of dissertation*
(Doctoral dissertation). Retrieved from Name of database.
(Accession or Order Number).

Lauro, S.J. (2011). *The modern zombie: Living death in
the technological age* (Doctoral dissertation). Retrieved
from Proquest Dissertations & Theses Global. Order No.
3482243.

A REVIEW

Last Name, First and Middle Initials. (Year, Month Day). Title of review. [Review of *Title of work*, by First and Middle Initials Last Name]. *Periodical or Journal Title, volume*, page, DOI or URL

Macon, C. (2018, May 30). "Monster portraits": An exploration of identity that's entirely unique. [Review of *Monster portraits*, by D. Samatar & S. Samatar]. *Los Angeles Review of Books*. https://lareviewofbooks.org/article/monster-portraits-an-exploration-of-identity-thats-entirely-unique#!

A PAGE ON A WEBSITE

Last Name, First and Middle Initials. (Year, Month Day). Site name. Retrieved from URL

Carrillo, S. (2014, October 28). Why we love monsters. Retrieved from http://lanetwork.facinghistory.org/why-we-love-monsters/

AN ARTICLE FROM AN ONLINE DATABASE

Last Name, First and Middle Initials. (Date of Publication). Title of article. *Title of Journal or Periodical, volume number*(issue number), page range. DOI or URL

O'Leary, P. (2015). Sacred fantasy in game of thrones. *Critical Quarterly, 57*(1), 6–19. DOI: http://dx.doi.org/10.1111/criq.12174

EMAIL

Do not include emails in your list of references. Do cite them parenthetically in the body of the text.

A TWEET

Last Name, First and Middle Initials. [Twitter username]. (Year, Month Day). Full title of tweet [Tweet]. Retrieved from URL

Frankenstein, V. [therealvictorfrankenstein]. (2018, October 31). The monster lives [Tweet]. Retrieved from https://twitter.com/ therealvictorfrankenstein/status/333666999234566?lang=en

A YOUTUBE VIDEO

Last Name, First and Middle Initials. [Screen name]. (Year, Month Day). *Title of video* [Video file]. Retrieved from URL

Daly, E. (2012, September 3). *Nightmare! The birth of Victorian horror: Dracula* (full programme, feat. Eileen Daly) [Video file]. Retrieved from https://www.youtube.com/ watch?v=88edGlW3DT4&t=208s

A FILM

For a film, APA curiously stipulates that references be listed under the name of the producer.

Producer Last Name, First and Middle Initials. (Producer) & Director Last Name, First and Middle Initials. (Director). (Year of Release). *Title of film* [Motion picture]. Country of Origin: Studio or distributor.

McKittrick, S. (Producer), Blum, J. (Producer), Hamm, Jr., E.A. (Producer), & Peele, J. (Producer & Director). (2017, January 24). *Get out* [Motion picture]. United States: Universal Pictures.

A TV PROGRAM

Writer Last Name, First and Middle Initials. (Writer), & Director Last Name, First and Middle Initials.(Director). (Date of broadcast or copyright). Title of episode [Television series episode]. In Producer First and Middle Initials Last Name (Producer), *Series title*. City, State of origin: Studio or Distributor.

Logan, J. (Writer), & Bayona, J.A. (Director). (2014, May 11). Night work [Television series episode]. In P. Harris, S. Mendes, J. Logan, & K. Richards (Producers), *Penny dreadful*. United States/United Kingdom: Showtime/Sky.

III. Sample References (APA)

- Lists of works cited and bibliographies are always organized alphabetically by the lead author's last name or the title of works with unknown authors. *They are never numbered.*
- The first line of each entry should be flush with the left margin. Second and subsequent lines should be indented half an inch. *Works cited lists and bibliographies should never be centered.*
- When a source has more than one author, all authors are listed last name first, followed by initials.
- If you have more than one source included by the same author, organize them chronologically from earliest to most recent. Include the author's name with each entry.

Asma, S.T. (2009). *On monsters: An unnatural history of our worst fears*. New York: Oxford University Press.

Cohen, J.J. (1996). Monster theory (seven theses). In J.J. Cohen (Ed.), *Monster theory: Reading culture* (pp. 3–25). Minneapolis, MN: University of Minnesota Press.

Daly, E. (2012, September 3). *Nightmare! The birth of Victorian horror: Dracula* (Full programme, feat. Eileen Daly) [Video file]. Retrieved from https://www.youtube.com/watch?v=88edGlW3DT4&t=208s

Logan, J. (Writer), & Bayona, J.A. (Director). (2014, May 11). Night work [Television series episode]. In P. Harris, S. Mendes, J. Logan, & K. Richards (Producers), *Penny dreadful*. United States/United Kingdom: Showtime/Sky.

Mathijs, E. & Sexton, J. (2011). *Cult Cinema: An Introduction*. Malden, MA: Wiley-Blackwell.

McKittrick, S. (Producer), Blum, J. (Producer), Hamm, Jr., E.A. (Producer), & Peele, J. (Producer & Director). (2017, January 24). *Get out* [Motion picture]. United States: Universal Pictures.

Riefe, J. (2016, August 3). Guillermo del Toro: "I love monsters the way people worship holy images." *The Guardian*. Retrieved from: https://www.theguardian.com/film/2016/aug/03/guillermo-del-toro-bleak-house-home-lacma-exhibit

Suzuki, E. (2017). Beasts from the deep. *Journal of Asian American Studies, 20*(1), 11–28. https://doi.org/10.1353/jaas.2017.0002

Weinstock, J.A. (2008). *The rocky horror picture show*. London: Wallflower Press.

Weinstock, J.A. (2012). *The vampire film: Undead cinema*. New York: Columbia University Press.

CUNNING METHODS OF SUFFERING (AKA CHICAGO MANUAL OF STYLE)

Chicago

The Chicago Manual of Style outlines a citation format that is used in some social science publications and by many journals that focus on history. Below is a brief overview of Chicago referencing the 17th edition.

I. How to Cite Material within the Body of the Text Using Chicago

As opposed to the parenthetical citation format used by MLA, Chicago style uses *notes*—either footnotes (which appear at the bottom of each page) or endnotes (which group all the notes together at the end of the essay). To cite from a source, a *superscript* (little number) is placed after the quotation or inserted material and each number then corresponds to a full citation. Insert your superscript at the end of a sentence or clause. The number usually follows end punctuation:

- In Mathias Clasen's study of horror, he proposes that, "The horror genre ... achieves its peculiar affective goal by targeting an evolved defense system, the fear system."[1]

The little "1" following the sentence is the superscript. It directs the reader to a corresponding footnote at the bottom of the page, or endnote at the end of the essay that supplies a complete citation. The easiest way to do this is to use the "insert note" function of most word processors.

II. Formatting Notes

When using the Chicago system, the first time you reference a given source, you provide a complete citation in a note. After that, supply a shortened citation for additional references to the same source. Typically, a bibliography is also included with the Chicago system.

A BOOK

1. First Name Last Name, *Title of Book* (Place of publication: Publisher, Year of publication), page number.

1. Mathias Clasen, *Why Horror Seduces* (New York: Oxford University Press, 2017), 9.

Shortened citation for additional references if your essay includes more than one source by the author:

2. Clasen, *Why Horror Seduces*, 32.

For the bibliography:

Last Name, First Name. *Title of Book*. Place of publication: Publisher, Year.

Clasen, Mathias. *Why Horror Seduces*. New York: Oxford University Press, 2017.

A CHAPTER IN AN EDITED COLLECTION OR ANTHOLOGY

1. First Name Last Name, "Title of Chapter," in *Title of Book*, ed. First Name Last Name (Place of publication: Publisher, Year), page range.

1. Jeffrey Andrew Weinstock, "Postmodernism with Sam Raimi (or, How I Learned to Stop Worrying About Theory and Love *Evil Dead*)," in *Fear and Learning: Essays on the Pedagogy of Horror*, eds. Aalya Ahmad and Sean Moreland (New York: McFarland & Company, 2013), 20.

Shortened citation for additional references if more than one source by the same author:

2. Weinstock, "Postmodernism with Sam Raimi," 25.

For the bibliography:

Last Name, First Name. "Title of chapter." In *Title of Book*, edited by First Name Last Name, page range. Place of publication: Publisher, Year.

Weinstock, Jeffrey. "Postmodernism with Sam Raimi (or, How I Learned to Stop Worrying About Theory and Love *Evil Dead*)." In *Fear and Learning: Essays on the Pedagogy of Horror*, edited by Aalya Ahmad and Sean Moreland, 19–39. New York: McFarland & Company, 2013.

AN ARTICLE OR ESSAY
IN A SCHOLARLY JOURNAL

1. First Name Last Name, "Essay Title," *Journal Title* volume, no. (Year): page.

1. Stephen Arata, "The Accidental Tourist: *Dracula* and the Anxiety of Reverse Colonization," *Victorian Studies* 33, no. 4 (1990): 622.

Shortened citation for additional references:

2. Arata, "Accidental Tourist," 635.

For the bibliography:

Last Name, First Name. "Essay Title." *Journal Title* volume, no. (Year): page range.

Arata, Stephen. "The Occidental Tourist: *Dracula* and the Anxiety of Reverse Colonization." *Victorian Studies* 33, no. 4 (1990): 621–45.

AN ARTICLE IN A MAGAZINE

1. First Name Last Name, "Title of Article," *Magazine Name*, Month Day, Year, page range.

1. Lev Grossman, "Zombies Are the New Vampires," *Time Magazine*, April 9, 2009, 161.

Shorted citation for additional references:

2. Grossman, "Zombies," 161.

For the bibliography:

Last Name, First Name. "Article Title." *Magazine Title*, Month Day, Year. (Note: with magazines, page numbers are included in notes but omitted from bibliographic entries.)

Grossman, Lev. "Zombies Are the New Vampires." *Time Magazine*, April 9, 2009.

AN ARTICLE IN A NEWSPAPER

Page numbers are usually not included with newspaper articles.

1. First Name Last Name, "Article Title," *Newspaper Title*, Month Day, Year.

1. Manohla Dargis and A.O. Scott, "At the Movies: Our Monsters, Ourselves," *The New York Times*, May 5, 2017.

Shortened citation for additional references:

2. Dargis and Scott, "At the Movies."

For the bibliography:

Last Name, First Name. "Article Title." *Newspaper Title*, Month Day, Year.

Dargis, Manohla and A.O. Scott. "At the Movies: Our Monsters, Ourselves." *New York Times*, May 5, 2017.

A DOCTORAL DISSERTATION
OR MASTER'S THESIS

1. First Name Last Name, "Title of Thesis or Dissertation" (Type of Source, University, Year), page.

1. Sarah J. Lauro, "The Modern Zombie: Living Death in the Technological Age." (PhD diss., University of California, Davis, 2011), 200.

Shortened citation for additional references:

2. Lauro, "The Modern Zombie," 200.

For the bibliography:

Last Name, First Name. "Title of Thesis or Dissertation." Type of Source, University, Year.

Lauro, Sarah J. "The Modern Zombie: Living Death in the Technological Age." PhD diss., University of California, Davis, 2011.

A REVIEW

1. First Name Last Name, "Title of Review," Review of *Title of Work*, by Name of Creator, *Title of Journal or Periodical* volume, no., Month Day, Year, page. URL.

1. Caro Macon, "'Monster Portraits': An Exploration of Identity That's Entirely Unique," Review of *Monster Portraits*, by Del Samatar and Sofia Samatar, *Los Angeles Review of Books*, May 18, 2018. https://lareviewofbooks.org/article/monster-portraits-an-exploration-of-identity-thats-entirely-unique#!.

Shortened citation for additional references:

2. Macon, "Monster Portraits."

For the bibliography:

Last Name, First Name. "Review Title." Review of *Title of Work*, by Name of Creator. *Title of Journal or Periodical*, Month Day, Year, URL.

Macon, Caro. "'Monster Portraits': An Exploration of Identity That's Entirely Unique." Review of *Monster Portraits*, by Del Samatar and Sofia Samatar. *Los Angeles Review of Books*, May 18, 2018. https://lareviewofbooks.org/article/ monster-portraits-an-exploration-of-identity-thats-entirely-unique#!.

A PAGE ON A WEBSITE

1. First Name Last Name, "Title of Web Page," Publishing Organization or Name of Website, publication, update/ access date, URL.

1. Stephanie Carrillo, "Why We Love Monsters," Facing History and Ourselves, October 28, 2014, http://lanetwork. facinghistory.org/why-we-love-monsters/.

Shortened citation for additional references:

2. Carrillo, "Why We Love Monsters."

Systems of Citing Sources

For the bibliography:

Last Name, First Name. "Title of Web Page." Publishing Organization or Name of Website. Publication, update/access date. URL.

Carrillo, Stephanie. "Why We Love Monsters." Facing History and Ourselves, October 28, 2014. http://lanetwork.facinghistory.org/why-we-love-monsters/.

AN ARTICLE FROM AN ONLINE DATABASE

1. First Name Last Name, "Title of Article," *Title of Journal or Periodical*, volume, no. (Month Day, Year): page range, DOI or URL.

1. Peter O'Leary, "Sacred Fantasy in *Game of Thrones*," *Critical Quarterly 57*, no. 1 (May, 2015): 6–19, DOI: http://dx.doi.org/10.1111/criq.12174.

Shortened citation for additional references:

2. O'Leary, "Sacred Fantasy in *Game of Thrones*," 322.

For the bibliography:

Last Name, First Name. "Title of Article." *Title of Journal or Periodical* volume, no. (Month Day, Year): page range, DOI or URL.

O'Leary, Peter. "Sacred Fantasy in Game of Thrones." *Critical Quarterly 57*, no. 1 (May 04, 2015): 6–19, DOI: http://dx.doi.org/10.1111/criq.12174.

EMAIL

1. First Name Last Name, email message to Jeffrey Weinstock, Month Day, Year.

1. Victor Frankenstein, email message to author, October 31, 2018.

Shortened citation for additional references:

2. Frankenstein, email message.

For the bibliography:

Do not include emails in your bibliography.

A TWEET

1. First Name Last Name, "Tweet in its entirety," Twitter, Month Day, Year, time, URL.

1. Victor Frankenstein, "The Monster Lives," Twitter, October 31, 2018, 12:01 a.m., twitter.com/victorfrankenstein/status/333666999234566?lang=en.

Shortened citation for additional references:

2. Frankenstein, "The Monster Lives."

For the bibliography:

Do not include tweets in your bibliography, unless extensively discussed in the paper.

Systems of Citing Sources

A YOUTUBE VIDEO

1. First Name Last Name, "Title of Video," YouTube video, running time, publication date, URL.

1. Eileen Daly, "Nightmare! The Birth of Victorian Horror: Dracula (Full programme, feat. Eileen Daly)." YouTube video, 51:04, September 3, 2012, https://www.youtube.com/watch?v=88edGlW3DT4&t=208

Shortened citation for additional references:

2. Daly, "Nightmare!"

For the bibliography:

Last Name, First Name. "Title of Video." YouTube video, running time, Month Day, Year. URL.

Daly, Eileen. "Nightmare! The Birth of Victorian Horror: Dracula," YouTube video, 51:04, September 3, 2012. https://www.youtube.com/watch?v=88edGlW3DT4&t=208s.

A FILM OR TV PROGRAM

1. First Name Last Name, *Title of Film or TV Program* (original release year; City: Studio/Distributor, medium release year), medium, run time.

1. Jordan Peele, *Get Out,* (2017; Los Angeles: Universal Pictures, 2018), DVD, 104 min.

For the bibliography:

Last Name, First Name, dir. *Title of Film or TV Program*.
Original release year; City: Studio/Distributor, medium
release year. Medium, run time.

Peele, Jordan, dir. *Get Out*. 2017; Los Angeles: Universal
Pictures, 2018. DVD, 104 min.

III. Sample List of Works Cited Chicago (17th edition)

Asma, Stephen T. *On Monsters: An Unnatural History of Our
Worst Fears*. New York: Oxford University Press, 2009.

Cohen, Jeffrey Jerome. "Monster Theory (Seven Theses)." In
Monster Theory: Reading Culture, edited by Jeffrey Jerome
Cohen, 3–25. Minneapolis: University of Minnesota Press,
1996.

Daly, Eileen. "Nightmare! The Birth of Victorian Horror:
Dracula," YouTube video, 51:04, Sept. 3, 2012. https://
www.youtube.com/watch?v=88edGlW3DT4&t=208s.

Peele, Jordan, dir. *Get Out*. 2017; Los Angeles: Universal
Pictures, 2018. DVD, 104 min.

Mathijs, Ernest and Jamie Sexton. *Cult Cinema: An Introduction*.
Malden, MA: Wiley-Blackwell, 2011.

Riefe, Jordan. "Guillermo del Toro: 'I love monsters the
way people worship holy images.'" *The Guardian*
(London, England), August 3, 2016. https://
www.theguardian.com/film/2016/aug/03/
guillermo-del-toro-bleak-house-home-lacma-exhibit.

Suzuki, Erin. "Beasts from the Deep." *Journal of Asian
American Studies* 20, no. 1 (2017): 11–28. https://doi.
org/10.1353/jaas.2017.0002.

Weinstock, Jeffrey Andrew. *The Rocky Horror Picture Show*.
    London: Wallflower Press, 2008.
---. *The Vampire Film: Undead Cinema*. New York: Columbia
    University Press, 2012.

OUIJA

THE FINAL METHOD OF CITING SOURCES IS VIA OUIJA BOARD.

Should you use this system? Ask the board.

CHAPTER 7

THE GREAT BEYOND...

NOW YOU KNOW WHY MAD SCIENTISTS HAVE CRAZY HAIR.
Writing can be both terrifying and exhilarating, and is almost always hard work! As with anything else though, if you find what you are doing interesting, it is a lot more enjoyable—so hopefully

you've had some fun with this guide *and* feel more comfortable with academic writing.

It doesn't end here of course. The more experiments you perform—and tweak and revisit—the more proficiency and control you develop. So, keep at it. We'll end with one more experiment and a request.

YOUR TURN

Draft a letter to yourself at the start of the course reflecting on your experience of your composition course.

What was your experience like? Did you meet your goals— why and why not? Where do you think you have improved the most? What do you still need to work on?

And now the request (for both students and instructors): like you, I'm constantly learning and trying to revise and improve my writing and materials. I would love to hear your thoughts about this guide to composition, and welcome suggestions for other types of assignments. If you had an experiment that turned out exceptionally well and would like it considered for inclusion in a future edition of this guide, pass it along. And if I omitted something important or maked a mistake, let me know that as well. Direct your feedback to madscientistsguide@gmail.com. Thank you!

ADDENDUM 1

A SUCCESSFUL EXPERIMENT!

THE ESSAY BELOW WAS SUBMITTED AS PART OF AN UNDER-
graduate honors seminar on monsters at Central Michigan
University in 2017. It provides a useful example of a thesis-driven
research paper with a close reading element. The citation system
being utilized is MLA. (Please note: this is an actual undergraduate student essay and there are edits that could be made, both
to the essay itself and to the works cited at the end! No students
were harmed in the creation of this essay.)

The Stigmatization of Mental Disorders in Psychological Thrillers

Katelyn Miller

In 2015, the National Survey on Drug Use and
Health reported that 43.4 million adults aged
18 or over that live in the United States were
diagnosed within the past year with a mental,
behavior, or emotional disorder ("Any Mental
Illness (AMI) Among U.S. Adults"). To put this
into another perspective, this means that 17.9
percent of all adults living in the United States
have been diagnosed with some form of a psychological disorder as stated in the *Diagnostic*

and *Statistical Manual of Mental Disorders.* Since many people enjoy watching movies about things that reflect either their own lives or people that they know, there have been many movies made that deal with either the main or supporting characters having a mental disorder. However, many of these movies do not accurately depict the mental disorders they show on screen, which can lead to the public misunderstanding the disorder or making hasty generalizations about people who have mental disorders. There are also many movies that dehumanize people with mental disorders, with the individuals in these films being treated like they are second-class citizens. This contributes to the stigmatization of mental disorders in our society. In order to better understand why it is important to accurately depict mental illness in movies, this paper will analyze portrayals of dissociative identity disorder in Alfred Hitchcock's *Psycho* and M. Night Shyamalan's *Split* to show that Hollywood depictions of people with mental illness either show inaccurate or sensationalized symptoms, how these inaccurate portrayals add to the stigma surrounding mental illness, and the importance of accurately portraying individuals with mental illness.

The introduction here is making clear why the topic matters.

······>

The argument is made clear and the primary texts to be addressed introduced.

······>

A Successful Experiment!

In 1960, Alfred Hitchcock's *Psycho* was released for the first time. The movie follows Marion Crane, a secretary from Phoenix, who is on the run after stealing $40,000 from a client of her employer. While traveling to where her boyfriend Sam lives, Marion stops at the Bates Motel in order to rest and to avoid driving in the heavy rain. It is at the motel that she meets Norman Bates, the man who is responsible for the upkeep and running of the motel, and who has a tendency to reference his mother quite a bit. During the film's famous shower scene, the audience sees a figure enter the bathroom and then proceed to stab Marion to death. Her body is then discovered by Norman, who sinks her body and car in a nearby swamp. The rest of the movie then follows Marion's sister and boyfriend as they try to figure out where Marion is by hiring a private investigator to look into her disappearance. However, the private investigator is also killed by the mysterious figure who appears to be a woman, which leads the audience to assume that it is Norman's mother. It is finally revealed, however, that Norman's mother has been dead for ten years and that he has been keeping her body in his house. At the end of the movie, a psychiatrist explains to his audience that the killer is technically Norman's mother. This is because the mother is his secondary personality that came out and did the killings while Norman remained unware about the killings taking place or his

While one must guard against excessive plot summary or plot summary that replaces analysis, basic plot summary helps make the analysis comprehensible to those who have not seen the film. Notice how present tense is used to explain what happens.

Notice how the quotation is incorporated into the paragraph.

············>

dressing up like his mother when he was killing someone.

Based on the evidence given in the film, it can be assumed that Norman Bates has dissociative identity disorder, a psychological disorder that is characterized by a "disruption of identity characterized by two or more distinct personality states" (*Diagnostic and Statistical Manual of Mental Disorders*). In the case of Norman Bates, he has two personality traits—himself and his mother. For most of the movie, the audience can mostly just see the personality of Norman interacting with the other characters, like the private investigator and Marion. The personality of Norman's mother only comes out when she becomes jealous of Norman's falling for another person and kills that person in response; this can be seen in the murder of Marion Crane. While the scenes with the mother's personality are limited, those few minutes that the mother personality can be seen are enough to add to the stigma surrounding people with mental illness, mainly adding to the stereotype that people with mental illness are violent criminals.

The portrayal of Norman Bates is especially troubling because "dissociative identity disorder, formerly known as multiple personality or split personality, has been misrepresented to a tremendously high degree in films.... [I]n most depictions of individuals with more than one personality ... the individuals are cast as psycho killers" (Indick 124–125).

When Hollywood depicts individuals with dissociative identity disorder as criminals, this sends a message to the audience that anyone who has been diagnosed with dissociative identity disorder is likely to be a violent criminal, even though this is simply untrue. In fact, as Pirkis argues, though "violent acts are far more likely to be committed by on-screen characters with mental illness than by other characters," this happens "at a rate much higher than occurs in real life" (528). This is unfair to individuals who actually have dissociative identity disorder because many individuals experience "significant distress or impairment in social, occupational, or other important areas of functioning" (*Diagnostic and Statistical Manual of Mental Disorders*). In other words, individuals with dissociative identity disorder already face sufficient barriers to the enjoyment of their lives without being subject to such extreme prejudice—and these barriers, if anything, make it even less likely for a person with the disorder to carry out the sort of criminal spree depicted in *Psycho*.

While *Psycho* not only adds to the stereotype that individuals that are diagnosed with mental disorders are basically dangerous killers, it also follows in other ways the Hollywood trend of not accurately depicting the experiences or symptoms of individuals with mental disorders. While the psychiatrist at the end of the movie explains Norman's behavior in the movie is a result of his dissociative identity

The transition here moves us from the preceding paragraph to a new topic.

disorder, Norman actually does not match many of the criteria needed to be diagnosed with this disorder. In fact, Norman differs from the criteria in three important ways. The first is that "people with DID do not mimic the personalities of specific individuals they know; they may adopt various personalities but not of someone who already exists" (Young 46). If Norman truly had dissociative identity disorder, his mother would not be one of his personalities. Having Norman's only other personality be that of his mother is completely inaccurate and misrepresents the actual development of secondary personalities in individuals with dissociative identity disorder.

The second reason that Norman does not fit the criteria for dissociative identity disorder is that, in a person who actually has the disorder, "different personalities do not dialogue with each other (in fact, the basic idea of dissociation is that different parts are split off from one another and avoid interaction, in some cases not even sharing memories)" (Young 46). There are many instances throughout the movie where Norman is heard having a conversation with the personality of his mother. One of these conversations is first seen towards the beginning of the movie when Norman is talking to his "mother" at the house about having Marion over for dinner. This is an inaccurate portrayal of what it is like for an individual to have dissociative identity disorder and what it is like having different persoalities and thus could lead viewers incorrectly to believe that an individual with this disorder has conversations with their other personalities (any one of which could be a killer).

The third and final way that Norman does not meet the criteria for having dissociative identity disorder is that "people with DID are typically not psychotic (do not have major breaks with reality) and would be unlikely to believe that an embalmed body is alive" (Young 46). The psychiatrist at end of the movie establishes that Norman developed dissociative identity disorder to deal with his guilt over killing his mother. It is due to this guilt that Norman removes his mother's body from her grave and embalms the body in order to preserve it longer. This leads to Norman having a psychotic break where he believes that he is actually talking to his mother (instead of just her dead body) and then leads to his developing his mother as a personality. As Young has stated, most individuals with dissociative identity disorder are not psychotic, and characterizing these individuals as being psychotic is a completely false and harmful claim. Thus, having Norman be psychotic is one of several ways in which Hollywood has taken liberties in presenting dissociative identity disorder.

An effective summation of the paragraph.

A more recent movie that also incorporates a character with dissociative identity disorder is M. Night Shyamalan's *Split*, which was released in January of 2017. The movie follows Casey and her classmates Claire and Marcia after the three of them are kidnapped by a man named Kevin Crumb. Like Norman Bates, Kevin has dissociative identity disorder and his psychiatrist has identified that Kevin has twenty-three different personalities. However, Kevin has an unseen twenty-fourth personality, called "The Beast," that is being worshipped by two of Kevin's other personalities. When Kevin's personality "Dennis" invites Kevin's doctor over things go downhill quickly for the three girls. "The Beast" personality takes over Kevin for the first time and he kills the doctor, Claire, and Marcia. "The Beast" also eats parts of Claire's and Marcia's bodies after he is done killing them. "The Beast" tries to then kill Casey but she is able to bring Kevin back to control before "The Beast" can kill her and then she escapes into an underground tunnel. "The Beast" takes control of the body and tries to kill Casey again, but he spares her life when he notices Casey's scars from her past suicide attempts. The movie ends with Casey escaping and Kevin hiding out, with three of his personalities taking control of his body and planning to take over the world.

The author here relates this discussion to what preceded it, thus making connections across the essay.

········>

Like *Psycho*, *Split* portrays a young man with dissociative identity disorder who has a personality that either kills or hurts the other characters around them. Unlike Norman

Bates, the audience can see Kevin's different personalities manifest throughout *Split*. While *Split* does get right that an individual who is diagnosed with dissociative identity disorder can have personalities that are different genders and ages, *Split* still follows the Hollywood stereotype of making one or more of the personalities into a killer. As Indick explains, "we've [already] seen dissociative identity disorder as an illness inevitably linked with serial killing" with movies like Brian De Palma's *Dressed to Kill* and *Raising Cain* and James Mangold's *Identity*, which all feature a murderous individual with dissociative identity disorder (125).

Example of the use of a signal phrase leading into a quotation.

The most implausible thing that *Split* does is give the personality of "The Beast" supernatural abilities. "The Beast" is seen climbing up walls and the ceiling and is not even injured when Casey shoots him multiple times. In fact, the bullet wounds do not even slow "The Beast" down, and it doesn't even appear that the shots even hurt him. While the movie is right that an individual's other personalities do not have to behave like the individual, *Split* has taken that fact to a whole other level. By making "The Beast" have supernatural qualities helps the audience not believe that "The Beast" (and by extension, Kevin) is a redeemable and relatable character.

Neither *Psycho* nor *Split* uses their cinematic appeal to inform and teach the audience about a mental disorder. Instead, they further contribute to the idea that "people with a mental illness can[not] recover [from their illness] or become productive members of society" (Stuart 100). Even though more than fifty years have passed between the release of *Psycho* and *Split*, both movies utilize the dissociative killer archetype as one of their main plot devices and do little to combat the stereotype that mentally ill people are dangerous to not only themselves but also to society. After looking at these two movies, it can be seen that Hollywood takes many liberties in its portrayals of individuals with dissociative identity disorder. The various ways that these two movies depict dissociative identity disorder do not accurately reflect the symptoms or experiences that people with the disorder go through and it further implies that individuals with the disorder are violent. These inaccurate portrayals of mental disorders further add to the stigma surrounding individuals with mental disorders. If Hollywood wants to portray mental disorders in various movies, it cannot do so just for the entertainment value—and it should not take liberties with the symptoms of the disorder being shown. If mental illness can be portrayed more sensitively and accurately, then the stigma surrounding mental health will begin to lessen, especially when it comes to the idea that people with mental disorders are violent criminals.

The conclusion sums up the preceding argument and emphasizes again its importance

Works Cited

"Any Mental Illness (AMI) Among U.S. Adults." *NIH,* https://www.nimh.nih.gov/health/statistics/prevalence/any-mental-illness-ami-among-us-adults.shtml. Accessed 21 November 2017.

"Diagnostic and Statistical Manual of Mental Disorders." *Dsm. psychiatryonline.org,* American Psychiatric Association, dsm.psychiatryonline.org. Accessed 21 November 2017.

Indick, William. *Psycho Thrillers: Cinematic Explorations of the Mysteries of the Mind.* McFarland & Company, Inc., Publishers, 2006.

Pirkis, Jane, et al. "On-Screen Portrayals of Mental Illness: Extent, Nature, and Impacts." *Journal of Health Communication,* vol. 11, no. 5, 2006, pp. 523–541.

Stuart, Heather. "Media Portrayal of Mental Illness and Its Treatments: What Effect Does It Have on People with Mental Illness?" *CNS Drugs,* vol. 20, no. 2, 2006, pp. 99–106.

Young, Skip Dine. *Psychology at the Movies.* Wiley-Blackwell, 2012.

A SUCCESSFUL EXPERIMENT!

THE FOLLOWING STUDENT ESSAY ON THE 2018 ADAPTATION of Stephen King's novel *It* is an example of a short thesis-driven essay that supports its argument through close reading. MLA citational formatting has been employed. (Please note: this is an actual sample of student writing and, as such, may not be perfect!)

Pennywise the Dancing Clown as a Metaphor for Bullying

Dimitri Dikhel

In Stephen King's horror novels, the supernatural often serves as a reflection of the more realistic problems that haunt the characters. For instance, in *Pet Sematary* (1983), both incurable afflictions and undeath are shown as examples of how "sometimes dead is better" (153), while Jack Torrence from *The Shining* (1977) is struggling both with alcoholism, an affliction that once made him break his son's arm, and ghosts that want him to kill his family. In Stephen King's *It*, the Losers Club is tormented both by a gang of bullies and by the eponymous monster. Although the way it assumes the form of Pennywise the Dancing Clown to lure in children is reminiscent of a child molester, ITs persistent mocking of the protagonists and feeding on their fear also makes it like a bully. In the 2018 adaptation of King's novel, Pennywise (Bill Skarsgård) is less discreet in his villainy than he was in the source material, or even the 1990 miniseries, and seems to relish the suffering of his victims more than in previous versions. Even more so than his book counterpart, this version of Pennywise seems to be a metaphor for bullying.

Pennywise's behavior towards the Losers Club makes him similar to Henry Bowers who, together with his friends, torments the members of the Losers Club. Henry is shown to be sadistic and does not hesitate when he is about to carve his name into Ben's belly. While Henry's friends die in the book after they join him in the sewers to attempt to kill the members of the Losers' Club, the 2018 film limits their involvement. Instead, Henry finds an ally in Pennywise, who shares his love of violence. They become two faces of the same problem: bullies who feed on the fear of their victims.

As with real-world bullies, the bullies in *IT* are assisted by the indifference of those who could help but do not. Adults in the film seem to be of little help, and bystanders doing nothing allow the bullies to get away with it. This parallel is established when Georgie dies at the beginning of the film and his screams attract an old woman. She sees blood, but instead of doing anything, she goes back inside—either out of fear, apathy or (as is oftentimes implied in the original novel) due to ITs influence. The exact same thing happens when Henry bullies the Losers Club members outside their school. Adults, including Henry's father who is a police officer, see what is going on but fail to intervene.

Near the end of the film, Pennywise gets a hold of Bill and offers to spare his friends if they will abandon Bill. As the film casts Pennywise as an exaggerated version of a bully, it also comments on how to best deal with bullying: solidarity among those affected. Rather than ignore the problem or to save themselves by abandoning their friend, the Losers Club fights back and, like all who prey on the weak, IT is shown to be a coward.

In the film, Pennywise squirms and fearfully shivers after its defeat, as Bill tells it, "Now you're the one who is afraid." However, IT is bound to return in the sequel, thus exemplifying how, although it is oftentimes shrugged off as a normal part of childhood, bullying can still leave a mark.

In what is a lucky coincidence, Andy Muschietti's 2018 adaptation of Stephen King's It came out twenty-seven years after the miniseries starring Tim Curry, just like the eponymous monster returns every twenty-seven years to feed. Although both Curry's and Skarsgård's performances as Pennywise are faithful to the novel, they emphasize different facets of the character, showing how the same story can teach different lessons and be adapted to suit different contexts. Skarsgård's Pennywise is a bully: he mocks and torments the children and, even before allying with him, he and Henry Bowers are shown to be similar. The film proposes that the thing that enables Pennywise and bullies to thrive is the indifference of those who see something but say nothing, and it suggests that, in the end, overcoming bullies and bullying requires solidarity among those affected.

Works Cited

It. Directed by Andy Muschietti, performances by Jaeden Lieberher, Bill Skarsgård, and Finn Wolfhard, Warner Bros. Pictures, 2017.

It. Directed by Tommy Lee Wallace, performances by Tim Curry, Harry Anderson, and Dennis Christopher, Warner Bros. Television, 1990.

King, Stephen. *It: A Novel*. 1986. Scribner, 2016.

---. *Pet Sematary*. 1983. Pocket Books, 2002.

---. *The Shining*. 1977. Pocket Books, 2002.

COMMON MAD SCIENTIST MISTAKES

(and How to Avoid Them)

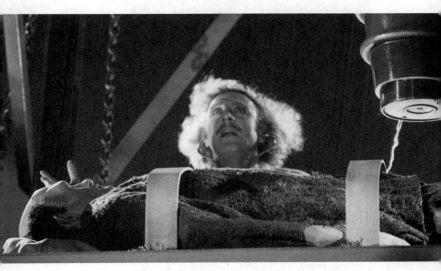

1. *Never* put an abnormal brain into your experiment!
2. Punctuation placement.

IN NORTH AMERICAN ENGLISH (AS OPPOSED TO THE BRITISH system), commas and periods come *between* quotation marks rather than after. The exception is when you are including a page number in parentheses. In this case, end punctuation is moved to follow the parentheses.

3. Quotation marks.

In the North American system, use double quotation marks except to indicate a quotation within a quotation.

4. Do *not* read Latin incantations aloud unless you know exactly what they mean!

5. Novels.

Novels are *extended works of fiction*. If it isn't fiction and/or if it isn't book-length, don't refer to it as a novel.

6. Titles.

- If something is a small part of something larger, you indicate the title by using quotation marks (double, not single). This applies to essays, articles, short stories, songs, subsidiary web pages, and so on. Ask yourself this: Is the source included in or on something else? If the answer is

yes, then use quotation marks (and just quotation marks—not quotation marks and italics).
- If something "stands alone"—is *not* a smaller part of something larger—use italics. This applies to titles of books, movies, main webpages, newspapers, journals, magazines, albums, and so on.
- Don't use underlining unless you are working on a manual typewriter.

7. The semicolon.

Only use a semicolon if you could put a period in its place. (The only exception here is a list of items that include commas, but this is unusual.)

8. In the event of a sudden change in cabin pressure, secure your oxygen mask first before assisting others.
9. The apostrophe.

Use the apostrophe to show that someone or something possesses something else.

10. Names.

Introduce authors by their full names the first time you mention them; after that, unless you know them personally, refer to them by their last names only.

11. Tense.

- When using the MLA system, use present tense to explain what an author says or what happens in a work or film.

- Use the past tense when making statements of historical fact.
- In the APA system, past tense is used to explain what an author says or what happens in a work or film.

12. Second person.

In general, avoid using the second person "you" in your writing unless you are really addressing your reader directly.

13. Do *not* call up that which you cannot put down again.

FINISHING TOUCHES

AS DISCUSSED IN CHAPTER FOUR, ALL WRITING IS IN SOME
respect *rhetorical*—that is, it seeks to persuade a reader to think,
feel, or act in particular ways. This is of course true of your writing
experiments here and elsewhere.

Different types of writing have different objectives, but
among the many goals student writers often have is a positive
evaluation from an instructor. With that in mind, here are some
"finishing touches" that can help inspire your instructor to think
kindly of you. While attending to these details won't offset lack-
luster content, they can help create a positive impression.

1. Formatting

Unless you have a time machine, you never get a second chance
at a first impression—and the very first thing that your instructor
will notice is whether you have paid attention to any formatting
instructions provided, so double-check this.

You really, really don't want your instructor's first impression
to be dismay or frustration, so make sure margins, font, font size,
spacing and so on conform to any provided instructions because
it is unfortunate to get docked points for something so easily
avoidable. And, unless you are told not to, be sure to include your
name on your work!

2. Titles

Your goal with any assignment is to make your reader *want to read* yours first. With that in mind, come up with a creative title. Avoid generic titles like "Essay Two" or "*Frankenstein* Essay." Imagine you have 100 essays to grade and think of a title that would make you want to read that paper first.

3. Spell-check, proofreading, and common mistakes

- Make sure to run spell-check, but remember there are many kinds of typos spell-check won't catch (and that spell-check can sometimes introduce problems, such as when it corrects your misspelling of "important" to "impotent" throughout your essay).

- Make sure to spell these things in particular correctly: your instructor's name, the names of people you discuss in your essay, and the titles of works you discuss in your essay. It is hard to convince a reader you know what you are talking about if you misspell the name of the author and/or text you are discussing!
- To catch other kinds of typos and errors, read your work out loud. I'm serious about this! Do it. Do it.
- And consult the "common mistakes" list that comes just before this addendum.

4. File names

Remember when uploading or emailing files to save files with names that identify them as yours. You know what "essay 1" is when it is in a course-specific folder on your computer; however, your instructor may receive many files with the same name and this can create confusion.

PERMISSIONS ACKNOWLEDGMENTS

Asma, Stephen T. "Monsters and the Moral Imagination," from *Chronicle of Higher Education*, October 25, 2009; 2461 words. As seen at https://www.chronicle.com/article/Monstersthe-Moral/48886

IMAGE CREDITS

PERMISSIONS ACKNOWLEDGMENTS

Page 30: Still from *The Blob*, 1958. Copyright © Worldwide Entertainment Corporation. Reproduced with permission.

Page 39: Bela Lugosi as the scheming Ygor resurrects Dr. Frankenstein's monster, played by Lon Chaney Junior, in the horror sequel *The Ghost of Frankenstein*, directed by Erle C. Kenton. (Photo via John Kobal Foundation/Getty Images.)

Page 41: Windigo image courtesy of mythology.wikia.org.

Page 42: iStock.com/Grafissimo

Page 44: Fredric March in *Doctor Jekyll and Mr Hyde*. (Photo by Hulton Archive/Getty Images.)

Page 47, left to right: iStock.com/Obradovic; iStock.com/SolStock; iStock.com/Rawpixel

Page 49, top to bottom: Google and the Google logo are registered trademarks of Google LLC; used with permission; LibrarySmartSearch reprinted with the permission of Central Michigan University Office of the General Counsel and the Associate Dean of University Libraries.

Pages 50–52: Reproduced by permission of the Modern Language Association.

Page 53: Theseus and the Minotaur on 6th-century BCE black-figure pottery. Image courtesy Wikimedia Commons, image by GreenMountainBoy.

Pages 54 and 59: Tenga, A. Screenshot of notes (page 85) from "Vampire Gentlemen and Zombie Beasts: A Rendering of True Monstrosity," in *Gothic Studies* 15.1, May 2013. Republished with permission of Manchester University Press via Copyright Clearance Center, Inc.

Page 55: iStock.com/koya79

PERMISSIONS ACKNOWLEDGMENTS

Page 100: The BADGER explosion on April 18, 1953, as part of Operation Upshot-Knothole, at the Nevada Test Site. Image courtesy of Wikimedia Commons.

Page 104: Still from *Frankenstein Meets the Wolf Man*. Copyright © 1943 Universal Pictures.

Page 105: Still from *Young Frankenstein* copyright © 1974 Twentieth Century Fox. All rights reserved.

Page 107: Still from *Young Frankenstein* copyright © 1974 Twentieth Century Fox. All rights reserved.

Page 108, top to bottom: iStock.com/Zbynek Pospisil; CBS/Getty Images

Page 113: "Jason Voorhees" by Andreh Santos on Flickr. This image is licensed under the Creative Commons Attribution-NoDerivs 2.0 Generic (CC BY-ND 2.0) license.

Page 114: Christopher Lee as the blood-sucking Count in *Dracula A.D. 1972*, directed by Alan Gibson for Hammer Films, 1972. (Photo by Silver Screen Collection/Hulton Archive/Getty Images.)

Page 131: iStock.com/johan63

Page 141: Still from *Young Frankenstein* copyright © 1974 Twentieth Century Fox. All rights reserved.

Page 150: iStock.com/D-Keine

Page 151: iStock.com/101cats

Page 152: Still from *L'attaque du monstre géant suceur de cerveaux de l'espace (The Attack of the Giant Brain-Sucking Monster from Space)*. Metronomic, 2010. Reprinted with the permission of Jérémy Rochigneux.

Page 154: iStock.com/gremlin

PERMISSIONS ACKNOWLEDGMENTS

INDEX

From the Publisher

A name never says it all, but the word "Broadview" expresses a good deal of the philosophy behind our company. We are open to a broad range of academic approaches and political viewpoints. We pay attention to the broad impact book publishing and book printing has in the wider world; for some years now we have used 100% recycled paper for most titles. Our publishing program is internationally oriented and broad-ranging. Our individual titles often appeal to a broad readership too; many are of interest as much to general readers as to academics and students.

Founded in 1985, Broadview remains a fully independent company owned by its shareholders—not an imprint or subsidiary of a larger multinational.

For the most accurate information on our books (including information on pricing, editions, and formats) please visit our website at www.broadviewpress.com. Our print books and ebooks are also available for sale on our site.

broadview press
www.broadviewpress.com

The interior of this book is printed on 100% recycled paper.